Gallery Books
Editor: Peter Fallon

UNCLE VANYA

Brian Friel

UNCLE
VANYA

*A version of the play
by Anton Chekhov*

Gallery Books

Uncle Vanya
is first published
simultaneously in paperback
and in a clothbound edition
on the day of its première,
6 October 1998.

The Gallery Press
Loughcrew
Oldcastle
County Meath
Ireland

ISBN 1 85235 236 1 (*paperback*)
      1 85235 237 X (*clothbound*)

The Gallery Press acknowledges the financial assistance of An Chomhairle Ealaíon / The Arts Council, Ireland, and the Arts Council of Northern Ireland.

Characters

ALEXANDER SERABRYAKOV, *retired professor*
ELENA, *his wife, aged 27*
SONYA, *daughter by his first wife, Vera Petrovna*
MARIA VOYNITSKY, *widow of a Privy Councillor and mother of the Professor's first wife*
VANYA (IVAN) VOYNITSKY, *her son, aged 47*
MIKHAIL ASTROV, *a doctor, aged 37*
ILYA TELEGIN, *an impoverished landowner*
MARINA, *on old nurse/nanny*
YEFIM, *watchman/retainer*
LABOURER, *on Serebryakov estate*

The action takes place on the Serebryakov estate.

Uncle Vanya, Brian Friel's version of the play by Anton Chekhov, was first produced by the Gate Theatre, as part of the Dublin Theatre Festival, on 6 October 1998, with the following cast:

ALEXANDER SEREBRYAKOV	T. P. McKenna
ELENA	Susannah Harker
SONYA	Donna Dent
MARIA VOYNITSKY	Ann Rowan
VANYA (IVAN) VOYNITSKY	Niall Buggy
MIKHAIL ASTROV	John Kavanagh
ILYA TELEGIN	Eamon Morrissey
MARINA	Daphne Carroll
YEFIM/LABOURER	Ciaran Reilly

Director	Ben Barnes
Set Designer	David Gaucher
Costume Designer	Jacqueline Kobler
Lighting Designer	Rupert Murray
Assistant to Director	Thomas Conway

Úna Ní Dhubhghaill provided the literal translation on which this version of *Uncle Vanya* was based.

ACT ONE

A garden. Part of the house and verandah can be seen. A table is set for tea under an old poplar tree. Chairs and garden seats. A guitar sits on one chair. Close to the table is a swing.

It is between 2.00 p.m. and 3.00 p.m. on a warm, overcast afternoon towards the end of the summer.

MARINA, *a heavy, slow-moving old woman, is sitting beside the samovar, knitting a stocking. astrov is walking up and down close by.* MARINA *puts aside her knitting and pours a glass of tea.*

MARINA Doctor.

ASTROV Yes?

MARINA A glass of tea.

ASTROV No, thanks. Not just at the — (*She thrusts the glass into his hand*) Thank you, Marina.

MARINA Or maybe a drop of vodka?

ASTROV I don't drink vodka *every* day, Marina. This is fine. How long have we known each other?

MARINA Oh Lord — my memory — When you first came to these parts, Sonya's mother was still alive, God be good to her.

ASTROV And very beautiful she was, wasn't she?

MARINA And she died nine years ago. So it must be eleven years, maybe more.

ASTROV Have I changed much in that time?

MARINA Oh, yes! You were young then. And handsome. Now you're neither young nor handsome.

ASTROV Thank you.

MARINA You weren't a vodka man then either.

ASTROV Of course you're right. In eleven years I've completely changed. Overworked, Nanny. Absolutely. On my feet from early morning until I stagger into bed at night and even then I lie there all

11

tensed up waiting for another call. In all the years we've known each other, not one day off — not a single day! And then you tell me I look ancient.

MARINA What I said was —

ASTROV Look at the lives people here live: they're stupid, they're boring, they're squalid. No, no — freakish — that's closer to it. I live among freaks. For God's sake I've become a freak myself! (*He pulls at his long moustache*) Look, Marina, look! Heehaw! Doctor Astrov — Doctor Asinine! Of course the brain still performs its routine little tasks; but all feeling, whatever emotional charges I once felt — dried up. There's nothing I want any more, nothing I need and no one in the world I have even a flicker of love for — with one exception of course. (*He kisses her on the head*) I had a nurse like you when I was a child.

MARINA Can I get you something to eat?

ASTROV Doctor Atrophied, that's me. Absolutely. There was a typhus epidemic in the village of Malitskoye just before Easter. I'd never seen squalor like that ever before: hovels filled with smoke — filth — the stench of decay — those low voices asking patiently for help — children dying on bare floors and pigs and sheep walking across them. I did what I could. Worked non-stop through the day without a bite to eat. And when I got home that night they had a signalman from the railway waiting to be operated on. I hadn't had a drink all day but I was in no state to — Anyhow I got him on the table to operate and he died under the anaesthetic. I thought: I have murdered this man! And for the first time in years every emotion, every instinct suddenly exploded into life and I was shaking with feeling. I just sat there and closed my eyes and waited until the trembling stopped. And I thought — I thought — all those generations that come after us, all those people we're preparing the way for, will they even remember us?

VANYA comes out of the house. He has been sleeping and looks rumpled. He sits on a bench and adjusts his smart tie.

VANYA Yes — yes, indeed —

ASTROV Had you a good sleep, Vanya?

VANYA Had I? I'm not sure. Ever since the Professor and his wife came to live here, the house has been turned upside down. I sleep at strange hours; I eat peculiar food; and I drink too much wine. Not good at all. Before they came to live here, life was firmly regimented — every day had a shape and a purpose. Sonya and I just worked from morning to night. Now Sonya works from morning to night and I just eat and sleep and drink. Not good at all.

MARINA He's right. The samovar's on the boil from early morning. But when does the Professor appear? Not until one o'clock. And then we have 'lunch'. One o'clock was always dinner-time, wasn't it? Now we don't have our dinner until seven o'clock — and that used to be tea-time! It's unnatural. D'you know what he does? Spends the whole night reading and writing and then in the middle of the night the bell rings. Tea, if you don't mind! Maybe at four in the morning!

ASTROV How long are they going to stay?

VANYA Forever. The Professor has decided this is going to be his home for ever and ever.

MARINA And now the samovar's been boiling for over two hours — and where are they? Gone for a walk! Is that natural?

The sound of voices off.

VANYA They're coming — they're coming — keep your

voice down —

SEREBRYAKOV, ELENA, SONYA *and* TELEGIN *enter.*

SEREBRYAKOV Exquisite countryside — exquisite — everywhere the eye falls — just exquisite.

TELEGIN (*To all*) He's right — exquisite. Exquisite, Professor. (*To all*) And very nice, too. Am I the only one feels that heat? The sweat's just lashing off me.

SONYA And on Sunday we'll go to the plantation, Father. We'll all go! Uncle Vanya?

VANYA Let's have tea first, Sonya. Elena?

SEREBRYAKOV I'll have mine in the study, if I may. Research calls, I'm afraid. Send it in, will you?

SONYA We'll bring a picnic and have it by the side of the lake.

SEREBRYAKOV, SONYA *and* ELENA *go into the house.* TELEGIN *sits beside* MARINA.

VANYA I didn't hear research calling — did you?

ASTROV Don't be a crank, Vanya.

VANYA It's hot and it's clammy and what does our great man of learning wear? Overcoat, galoshes, gloves, a scarf.

ASTROV He looks after himself, Vanya, that's all.

VANYA But isn't she beautiful? (*Savours the name*) Elena. She is the most beautiful woman I have ever laid eyes on.

TELEGIN When I go for a walk in the country, Marina, or drive through the woods, or just — just — just gaze at that table there, I experience — how can I put it? — an ecstasy that is beyond words!

MARINA God save us!

TELEGIN Look at that sky! Listen to those birds! We are all so happy together — in such — such accord! Could we ask for anything more?

MARINA (*Offering a glass*) Tea.

TELEGIN Just what I need. Am I the only one's destroyed?

VANYA (*Dreamily*) Now *that's* exquisite.

ASTROV Hello, Vanya. (*Clicks his finger*) Vanya?

VANYA Yes?

ASTROV Talk to us.

VANYA What about?

ASTROV What's happening? What's new?

VANYA Nothing's happening. Nothing's new. I'm getting older. I'm getting crankier. I'm getting lazier. And then I look at my old mother, deaf as a post and one foot in the grave and bursting with enthusiasm for women's emancipation and protest meetings and all sorts of revolutionary causes. She really believes all those solemn pamphlets she reads. She really believes a new order is about to happen.

ASTROV Isn't she lucky? And the Professor?

VANYA My brother-in-law is — let's be exact about this, Mikhail — my brother-in-law is an oaf. A retired oaf. A fossilized oaf. An oaf with gout, rheumatism, migraine and a liver swollen with jealousy and frustration. An oaf who lives on the estate of my sister, his first wife, not because he likes it here, but because he can't afford to live in the town on his pension. An oaf who somehow acquired a degree and somehow got a university chair and for twenty-five years somehow, somehow tricked thousands of students into scribbling down the rubbish he lectured on art. On art! He knows as much about art as I know about — about surgery! For twenty-five years! And now that the oaf is retired, he's forgotten, and all that lecturing and all that furious research and all those vapid publications and essays — vanished! — buried! — never happened! Not a trace of the oaf exists!

ASTROV (*To* MARINA) Might one suspect that Vanya is perhaps just a little envious of the Professor?

VANYA Of course I am! Women adore him — can you

believe it? All women. His first wife, Vera Petrovna, my beautiful, gentle, angelic sister who had more admirers than he had students, she thought he was Jupiter and Adonis rolled into one. That oaf — Adonis!

ASTROV   (*To* MARINA) Perhaps just a teeny bit?

VANYA   My own mother, the oaf's mother-in-law, she's in awe of him! Can you believe it?— awed by *that*? His second wife, the exquisite Elena, she married him when he was already half-fossilized and at a stroke threw away her youth and her freedom and her — her — her luminosity. Why? Why? For God's sake, tell me why!

ASTROV   Is she faithful to him?

VANYA   Unfortunately.

ASTROV   Is that unfortunate?

VANYA   Because that sort of faithfulness is bogus. And it's bogus because it sounds 'worthy' but in fact it's stupid. To deceive an old husband you can't stand any longer — they say that's immoral. But to suffocate your youth and your natural passion and your hunger for life, is that a moral, a 'worthy' thing to do?

TELEGIN   Vanya — Vanya — I'm sorry — I just can't let that go unchallenged. Anybody who betrays a wife or a husband is equally capable of betraying his country as well. We're talking of high treason here. Sorry.

VANYA   (*Wearily*) Oh for God's sake, Waffles.

TELEGIN   No, I'm serious, Vanya. The day after we were married my wife ran off with another man.

ASTROV   Good God!

TELEGIN   A German. Hans. Charming man. Great horseman. Do you see your German? Remarkable race. Anyhow she decided suddenly she'd gone off my appearance. But to this day I still love her; I'm still faithful to her; I give her all the financial help I can afford; and I've spent all my money on the education of our children — well, her children — well, their children. What did I lose? Any chance of happiness in this life — of course I did. But what have I held on to? My dignity, Vanya. My pride. And what did she lose? Everything — her looks, her self-esteem, finally Hans. A big, big dip. So I ask you, Vanya: who came out very much on top? Doctor?

ASTROV (*Speechless*) Yes — indeed — I see —

SONYA *and* ELENA *enter. And in a short time* MARIA VOYNITSKY *engrossed in a pamphlet. She sits. She is handed a glass of tea which she accepts without looking up from her reading.*

SONYA There are some villagers at the back door, Nanny.
MARINA Villagers!
SONYA See what they want, will you? I'll look after this (*tea*).

MARINA *exits.* ELENA *takes her glass and sits on the swing.*

ASTROV (*To* ELENA) I got your note that the Professor wasn't well and here I am.
ELENA He wasn't well last night.
ASTROV Seems fine to me. You think it's gout?
ELENA His legs were aching. But he is much better today.
ASTROV (*Mock heroic*) The very second your note arrived I galloped here at break-neck speed.
ELENA Thank you.
ASTROV As I have done before. As you know.
ELENA Indeed.
ASTROV (*To* SONYA) And now that I'm here may I cadge a bed for the night?
SONYA You couldn't be more welcome. Have you had anything to eat?
ASTROV I'm afraid I just dashed off before —
SONYA You'll eat with us then. We now have dinner

about half-past six — at tea-time, as Nanny insists. (*Drinks*) This tea's cold.

TELEGIN At this time of year your air-temperature is a very volatile man. And your samovar can't cope with that. So your air-temperature just dances rings round him.

ELENA It's fine, Ivan. We'll drink it cold.

TELEGIN With respect, my name is not Ivan.

ELENA I'm sorry — ?

TELEGIN Ilya Ilyitch Telegin. Waffles to intimates.

ELENA Waffles?

TELEGIN Because of my pock-marked face. Lost me my wife as a matter of fact; that (*face*) and a little weakness all the Telegins suffer: victims to perspiration. Lost her to a German. Hans. Marvellous race, your German. Turn their hands to anything. Incidentally I am Sonya's godfather — (SONYA *blows him a kiss*) — and Professor Serebryakov, your distinguished husband, knows me since the old days. As a matter of fact I live here on your estate — ever since my fortunes took a little dip some years ago. As fortunes do. Live here and eat in this house every evening. In the kitchen. Indeed, madam, without Sonya and Vanya I'd be —

SONYA Without Ilya Ilyitch, Sonya and Vanya would be lost. He is our grip on reality. (*To* TELEGIN) Did you hear? The hay-maker's coming next Monday.

VANYA Is it?

TELEGIN Good.

VANYA Oh, God!

TELEGIN Great.

SONYA If the rain holds off.

VANYA Hay-making time — whoopee!

MARIA Where is your father, Sonya?

SONYA In the study, Grandma. (*Louder*) In the study.

MARIA He'll want to see this — Pavel Alekseyevich's latest political pamphlet. He sent me a copy.

ASTROV Interesting?

MARIA What?

ASTROV Is it interesting?

MARIA Disgraceful! He's attacking the very positions he was defending seven years ago!

VANYA So he changed his mind.

MARIA Just abandoned every revolutionary principle he ever had.

VANYA That's shocking. Just drink your tea, Mother.

MARIA Don't patronise me, young man. I may express an opinion, may I not?

VANYA For fifty long years we have been expressing opinions and reading pamphlets and debating and arguing. Now it's time to enjoy cold tea.

MARIA So I'm not allowed to speak in my own house? Oh, dear!

VANYA Mother, you may —

MARIA Abandoning one's principles seems to be fashionable nowadays. What became of the man who had convictions, staunch beliefs, who knew exactly —

VANYA — where he stood on every issue. Indeed, what became of him? Until twelve months ago he was like you, Mother: the very essence of life could be found in a pamphlet or in a cause or in a political belief. Chaff, Mother. Trumpery. Guff. Smoke. The essence of life isn't there. I know that now, and now — now that it's too late — now I'm eaten up with fury and with frustration because I've wasted my life, because I'm now too old to pursue the things — the real things — I might have had. Oh, Mother, if you only knew the force of that fury and that frustration.

SONYA No lectures, Uncle Vanya, please.

MARIA Can't hear a word he says. But of course his argument is specious. Principles, convictions are only guidelines. They must be translated into revolutionary action. But action was never your forte, was it?

VANYA What is my mother asking of me?

MARIA What is he saying?

VANYA Does she want me to become a writing-machine like her professor son-in-law?

MARIA I heard that! Are you suggesting — ?

SONYA Grandma! Uncle Vanya! Please!

VANYA (*To* SONYA) In deference to my niece — silence and apologies.

Pause.

ELENA The sun's trying to come out.

TELEGIN As if things aren't bad enough! (*To* ELENA) Do you sweat much yourself?

ELENA Good for the hay.

VANYA Oh, God — the hay! — the hay! — tra-la-la!

ELENA It will be a nice afternoon after all.

VANYA To swing maybe? (*He holds his head to the side as if he were hanged*)

TELEGIN *plays chords on the guitar.* MARINA *walks across the lawn.*

MARINA Chook-chook-chook-chook-chook-chook-chook.

SONYA What did the villagers want, Nanny?

MARINA That old squabble about the common ground down beside the lake. They're going to submit a 'discussion document' on it next week.

ASTROV A what?

MARINA And not one of them can write! Chook-chook-chook-chook.

SONYA Is there a hen missing?

MARINA The old speckled one has led her chicks away again. If I don't find them the magpies will. Chook-chook-chook-chook —

She goes off.

VANYA The old speckled hen — is she somehow — symbolic?

SONYA Behave yourself.

VANYA Chook-chook-chook-chook.

TELEGIN *plays a polka. They all listen in silence. A* LABOURER *enters.*

LABOURER Excuse me —

SONYA Yes?

LABOURER I'm looking for the Doctor, Miss.

ASTROV Yes?

LABOURER There's been an accident in the factory, Doctor. They want you to come immediately.

ASTROV Why?

LABOURER It's urgent, Doctor.

ASTROV It's always urgent, isn't it? All right — all right — all right — I'm coming — I'm coming.

TELEGIN He's a saint, really, your Doctor. But that's the way: no rest for the wicked.

ASTROV Get me a vodka from the kitchen — a large vodka.

The LABOURER *exits.* ASTROV *looks around.*

Well — a short visit — and I didn't even get examining my patient. (*To* ELENA) If you're at a loose end some day, why don't you call on me? Sonya, too, of course. I've a small estate — eighty acres or so; a few beehives; a nursery; and a model orchard — my pride and joy. And next to my place there's a government plantation. And the forester there is so old that I — I suppose I run the whole thing.

ELENA Sonya tells me you're passionate about trees.

ASTROV Am I?

ELENA But medicine is your real vocation, isn't it?

ASTROV Is it?

ELENA It interests you more?

ASTROV Medicine?

ELENA Forestry.

ASTROV Maybe.

VANYA (*Ironically*) Full of dark passions.

ASTROV (*To* ELENA) You look surprised. Forestry is fasci-
nating.

VANYA (*Ironically*) Utterly.

ASTROV You don't believe me.

ELENA It's just that you're a young man —

ASTROV Is thirty-seven young?

ELENA All right — you're ancient. But I'd have thought
that even at your time of day there might be
something more exciting in your life than —
sitka spruce. A 'government plantation' hasn't
exactly the ring of a fun-fair, has it?

SONYA Wait till you see his nursery and his model
orchard. I know it sounds strange but they are
thrilling!

VANYA 'Absolutely'.

SONYA (*To* ASTROV) We'll go over as soon as the hay is
saved.

VANYA Tra-la-la — tra-la-lee.

SONYA What is the matter with you, Uncle Vanya? (*To*
ELENA) What he is doing is protecting the old
forests from destruction and at the same time
he's planting every acre he can get his hands on.
He was Forester of the Year last year! He'll show
you his silver medal.

ASTROV Bronze.

SONYA He got a prize for his bee-keeping, too. And he's
not just an amateur enthusiast — he has worked
out a whole philosophy about arboriculture. (*To*
ASTROV) I looked it up — aboriculture. Isn't that
the word?

ASTROV Sounds impressive.

SONYA You see, Mikhail believes that forests are not just
magnificent things in themselves — that they
adorn the earth — that they inspire in us a sense
of awe, a sense of the spiritual — of course they
do. But he also believes — amn't I right, Mikhail?

ASTROV He believes what?

SONYA Now he's embarrassed. He believes that forests make a harsh climate milder. That is a scientific fact, he says. And the milder your climate, the less energy you spend battling with nature. And the less energy you spend battling with nature, the *more* energy you have to pursue gentler, more civilised habits. And the more gentle and more civilised people become, naturally the more sophisticated their thoughts, the more eloquent · their speech, the more graceful their movements — indeed the more beautiful they become. Honestly! It all sounds like an incredible leap from planting more trees — I know — I know. But it has a perfect logic, hasn't it? Just encourage that milder climate with your forests and eventually — eventually — a society will evolve where learning will blossom and people will become hopeful again and men will treat women more gently and with a little more consideration. (*She laughs — embarrassed at her passion*) Now I'm embarrassed. Sorry, Mikhail. I'm sure that's a complete distortion of what you think.

ELENA (*To* ASTROV) Is it?

VANYA (*Laughing*) Bravo — bravo! Sentimental nonsense, Sonya, but the passion is enviable. (*To* ASTROV) And I'm afraid I'll go on burning logs in my stoves and building my outhouses with wood.

ASTROV Burn turf in your stoves, Vanya. Build your outhouses with stone. You know yourself the forests of this country are being systematically raped.

VANYA Good God, by me?

ASTROV Every year thousands, millions of trees are cut down. Does that matter? You know it does. Our climate is being tampered with in a way we don't understand at all. A magnificent landscape is mutilated forever. Our rivers grow shallower and ultimately will dry up. And the natural habitat of animals and birds is so disturbed that they may never be reinstated. We are supposed to

23

be people of reason, creative people. But is it reasonable, is it creative to destroy what *we* cannot create? — to raze our forests, exterminate our wildlife, ruin our water supplies, damage our climate? Sentimental nonsense? I don't think so. A private obsession? Maybe. (*He shrugs*) No, it's not! Sometimes I walk along the perimeter of one of the forests I'm fighting to save, or listen to the whisper of young saplings I've planted with my own hands. Then I think — I *know* — that I have a tiny, tiny share in adjusting our climate; and if in a thousand years' time people are just that tiny, tiny bit happier, then I know it may be due in part to my tiny, tiny efforts. So that every time I plant a young birch and watch it turn green and grow tall and dance with the wind, all I can say is that I feel — no, not a tiny, tiny bit — but enormously, immoderately, inordinately *proud*! So there!

The LABOURER *appears with the vodka on a tray.* SONYA *applauds briefly and stops abruptly because nobody joins her.*

(*To* ALL) And the Doctor exits to thunderous applause. Look at those faces! A private obsession isn't a public crime, is it?

He goes towards the house. SONYA *rushes to his side and takes his arm.*

SONYA Great, Mikhail! Terrific! (*Aloud*) When are we going to see you again?
ASTROV Whenever, I suppose.
SONYA Have we to wait again for another whole month?

They go into the house. MARIA *and* TELEGIN *stay where they are.* ELENA *and* VANYA *move towards the verandah.*

VANYA 'God and the Doctor we alike adore / But only when in danger, not before.'

TELEGIN (*Fanning himself*) I seem to be the only one that's lashing.

MARIA (*Sternly*) Do you have to keep giving us these reports on your condition?

TELEGIN Family weakness, Maria. The wife found it very difficult, too — that and of course this (*face*).

ELENA When you are in one of your difficult moods, Vanya, you can be very disagreeable.

VANYA What are you talking about?

ELENA You hurt your mother with the talk of a non-stop writing-machine — you know you did. And you deliberately set out to pick a fight with Alexander at lunch-time. You can be a petty little man at times.

VANYA I think I hate your husband.

ELENA More vindictive than petty. And you have no reason to hate him. He's just the same as the rest of us — no better, no worse. Don't be so judgemental.

VANYA If you could only see your face and the way you move: so languorous, such weariness of us all. We bore you to death, don't we?

ELENA Attacking Alexander is so easy it is just tiresome. And then that cloying pity for me: poor Elena, married to that old man; how sorry we are for her. For God's sake, that's a bit transparent, isn't it? Just as Mikhail was saying, men's first response is to destroy. That forest there — cut it down. Those birds — shoot them. That woman — she's not mine but I want her. Sorry, can't have her. Who cares? She's disposable; there's always another. Woods — wildlife — women — use them — abuse them — discard them. I thought you were a bigger man than that.

VANYA These are silly generalisations, Elena, and in your heart —

ELENA He looks tired, anxious, doesn't he?

VANYA Who?

ELENA Mikhail. But such an interesting face.

VANYA And you're unfair to me — and to yourself — when you say —

ELENA Not hard to see why Sonya's in love with him. And she's so inept at concealing it. He has been here three times since we came to live here but I haven't had a real talk with him yet. But a man as engaged and as passionate as that wouldn't have much to say to me. Vanya, you and I have one thing in common.

VANYA Just one?

ELENA We are both dreary, uninteresting people. Don't look at me like that. I've told you I don't like it.

VANYA How else can I look at you since I love you, Elena? You are the only happiness I know. You are the joy of my life. You are my youth, Elena. I know — I do know — that there is no possibility that you might love me, might ever come to love me. But please, please just let me gaze at you, listen to your voice —

ELENA Shhhhh! They'll hear you, Vanya.

She moves towards the house. He follows her.

VANYA Let me tell you how much I love you, Elena — that's all. Just let me speak. Just to be allowed to tell you — just to look at you — just to be in your presence —

ELENA For God's sake, Vanya!

She quickly goes into the house. He follows her. TELEGIN plays a polka. Stops. Mops his forehead.

TELEGIN Late summer is a treacherous time. If your storm isn't on top of you, he's on his way.

MARIA Pavel Alekseyevich.

TELEGIN Who's that?

MARIA Why did we ever trust him?

She holds an imaginary revolver to her temple and shoots.

We're far too tolerant.

She plunges into her pamphlet again.

TELEGIN We'll have no more of your treason from you, Pavel Alekseyevich. By God, we won't. Do you sweat much yourself?

She does not hear him. She makes an important note on the margin of her pamphlet. TELEGIN *resumes his playing. End of Act One.*

ACT TWO

Some days later. The dining-room in Serebryakov's house. Night-time. SEREBRYAKOV *is lying back in an armchair. He is asleep.* ELENA, *sitting on an upright chair close to him, is dozing. In the distance* YEFIM, *the night-watchman, is singing a haunting peasant song. Suddenly* SEREBRYAKOV *wakens — in confusion, in panic, in terror.*

SEREBRYAKOV What? — What? — What? — Oh Jesus! — Who? — Who? — What? —

ELENA Shhh. It's all right.

SEREBRYAKOV What's that sound? — What's that noise? —

ELENA It's the night-watchman, singing.

SEREBRYAKOV What? — What? — Who ? —

ELENA Yefim — Yefim, the night-watchman. You slept for a while.

SEREBRYAKOV I must have slept for a while.

> SEREBRYAKOV *jumps to his feet and goes to the open window.*

(*Shouts*) Will you shut up out there? Just shut up, will you! What time is it?

ELENA Twenty past twelve.

> *He falls back into his seat.* YEFIM *continues.*

SEREBRYAKOV Drunken bloody louts going home from the pub.

ELENA I'll close the window.

SEREBRYAKOV Leave it open — I can hardly breathe. Did I doze off there?

ELENA You slept for an hour.

SEREBRYAKOV I dreamed that my left leg didn't belong to me but I could still feel pain in it, an excruciating

pain all down that side, more like rheumatism
than gout. Oh my God, why can't I breathe?

ELENA You're exhausted. This is the second night
you've had no sleep.

She fixes the rug around his knees again.

SEREBRYAKOV Leave me alone.

ELENA You'll get cold.

SEREBRYAKOV Stop fussing! I can do that myself. I hate being
old — hate it — hate it. Being old is disgusting —
even more disgusting to everybody around you.
And particularly disgusting to you, Elena; a sort
of personal, intimate disgust to you.

ELENA We all grow old, Alexander.

SEREBRYAKOV Now there's a profundity! 'We all grow old' —
hah! I do understand why I disgust you, Elena:
you're young and good-looking and hungry for
life. And look what you're spancelled with —
this old carcass. That's a particularly cruel
smothering of the spirit, isn't it? But be patient,
Elena. Just hang on a bit longer and I'll die and
you will live again.

She gets up and moves away.

ELENA Please, Alexander — please —

SEREBRYAKOV And you will console yourself that you looked
after me dutifully, indeed given your innate disgust for me you were wonderfully compassionate and really, really *almost* loving. And could an
old man ask for more than — almost love?

ELENA Please stop, Alexander. I don't think I can take
any more.

SEREBRYAKOV I'm sorry — that's stupid — I'm sorry. But a curious thing, isn't it, that when Vanya says something stupid, or that old fool, his mother, the
Princess of the Pamphlets, my mother-in-law, let
them speak and there's a reverential silence. But

when I open my mouth, all eyes are glazed. Especially curious considering that I earned my living and supported you handsomely with my 'talking'. He's (*Yefim*) doing that to defy me.

The window bangs.

ELENA I'll have to shut it — the wind's getting up.

She goes to close the window.

And there's going to be more rain. Yefim, please —

YEFIM *stops singing.*

SEREBRYAKOV I'm puzzled by it all. I had a privileged life; I know I had; and I'm grateful for it. Privileged and completely fulfilling. Mental stimulation, intellectual excitement; publications, success, fame. And I relished every second of it. And this is where it all ends up, on a broken-down estate: gossip, squabbling, stupidity — Yefim, for God's sake! (*He begins to cry*) My life is over, Elena, and I didn't experience any of it. It — it eluded me. I regret my entire existence, Elena. And I'm frightened of dying. Do you hear what I'm saying? Terrified.

ELENA I do know that. But in five or six years' time I'll be old too.

SONYA *enters.*

SONYA I'm cross with you, Father. You ask us to send for Doctor Astrov and now that he's here you won't let him look at you.

SEREBRYAKOV Doctor Vodka.

SONYA That's very selfish of you.

SEREBRYAKOV Your Doctor Astrov knows as much about medicine as I know about astronomy.

SONYA Do you want us to get the whole medical faculty out here to look at you?

SEREBRYAKOV I will not be treated by a woodcutter.

SONYA Fine — fine — suit yourself. As you always do.

SEREBRYAKOV I can't get a breath. Those drops on the table, Sonya.

SONYA These?

SEREBRYAKOV Not those — not those! The green bottle — green — green — green! Do you know what green looks like?

SONYA That'll do, Father. Just stop that bullying — all right? I'm not taking any more of it.

She goes to the window.

SEREBRYAKOV I ask for medication. Is that bullying?

SONYA Oh my God, it's pouring again!

ELENA It's been threatening all night.

SONYA (*Ignores her*) And the hay-maker's due at dawn! Oh my God!

Enter VANYA *in a dressing-gown. He has a glass in one hand, a candle in the other. He is slightly tipsy.*

It's pouring, Uncle Vanya! Look!

VANYA I know, and there's going to be a storm.

SONYA The hay, Uncle Vanya! The hay!

VANYA I'm afraid the hay won't —

SONYA The hay-maker's coming at daybreak!

VANYA (*Secretly relieved*) Maybe by then —

SONYA It won't even be able to get into the fields! (*A flash of lightning*) Oh my God!

VANYA It won't last. That's a promise. We *will* save that damned hay, Sonya. Now, you two, off to bed. Night-nurse is here.

SEREBRYAKOV For God's sake, I'm not going to be left alone with him, am I? He drives me mad with his ranting and his whingeing.

VANYA   Don't be selfish, Alexander. They sat up last night. Tonight's my turn.

SEREBRYAKOV   I don't need anybody. All of you go to bed. I'm perfectly well, thank you very much.

VANYA   Are you? Now that's good news.

SEREBRYAKOV   Everybody, please, out, out.

VANYA   And you look much better, too. Doesn't he look stronger?

SONYA   Uncle Vanya!

SEREBRYAKOV   Elena, take him with you, please.

VANYA   Take him, Elena. Please take him with you.

MARINA *enters. She is carrying a candle.*

SONYA   Nanny, what are you doing up?

MARINA   The tea things haven't been cleared away, have they? Who's going to do that?

SEREBRYAKOV   (*Shouts*) For God's sake, could I have a little peace? My head's exploding! Sonya'll do the damned tea things — Elena — I'll do them myself, for God's sake!

MARINA *goes to him.*

MARINA   Your legs are aching, aren't they? I know. You just want to cut them off, don't you? I have those pains, too, especially at night, especially if I've been on my feet all day. (*Arranges the rug around his knees*) It's the same trouble you had with those veins away back in the old days, isn't it? Vera Petrovna, may she rest in peace, I remember her crying with worry about them. Because she could do nothing to relieve you. Yes, crying real tears. I'd almost forgotten that. You were her whole life, you know; you and Baby Sonya. (*To* SONYA) You wouldn't remember that. (*To* SEREBRYAKOV) Isn't life strange? (*Briskly*) That's better. (*She kisses him on the shoulder*) Now, what's going to happen is this. Nobody's going to sit up tonight because we're all exhausted, and you're going to sleep in your own bed — lean on this arm — will someone take the other arm? — (SONYA *takes it*) and I'm going to make you some lime-flower tea and I'll bring you up a bed-warmer and before you know you'll be fast asleep and tomorrow morning the pains in the legs will be gone and you'll be as good as new and you and I'll be fit to do a polka together. Are we off?

SEREBRYAKOV Thank you, Marina. The only civilised voice in this house.

MARINA People think it's only the young ones who need a bit of attention. But old people can do with a bit, too. Now, amn't I the wise old woman?

MARINA, SEREBRYAKOV *and* SONYA *exit together.*

ELENA I can hardly stand. That man has me worn out.

VANYA And I wear myself out. Haven't closed an eye for three whole nights.

ELENA It's a very unhappy house this, Vanya. As if you don't know. Your mother hates everything except her pamphlets and the Professor. The Professor's a very ill man —

VANYA What's this — 'the Professor'? You mean 'my husband', don't you?

ELENA He doesn't trust me and he's afraid of you.

VANYA (*Mocking*) Terrified!

ELENA Sonya's so irritable with him — I don't know why. With me, too. Why is that? One minute she ignores me, the next she's hugging me. And I'm so wound up, so tense, I could burst into tears any moment. Not a very happy house, is it, Vanya?

VANYA But summarized perceptively and succinctly.

VANYA *drinks his glass and fills it again.*

ELENA You're the perceptive one, Vanya; the educated one. You know that it isn't the great battles that cause the most injury. It's all these petty squabbles, these corroding jealousies, these small domestic hatreds that eat away at our lives. You could change the whole atmosphere here if you stopped complaining and helped us to be reconciled to what we have.

VANYA If I could only be reconciled to myself. (*He grasps her hand*) My darling —

ELENA (*Pulling away*) Please, Vanya, please.

    Pause.

VANYA Oh, yes, the storm will break and the storm will pass and the world will be miraculously verdant and hopeful again. A fresh creation. Hope restored. It's that belief that sustains us, isn't it? But what if you have lost that belief, Elena? Or never had it. I don't think I ever believed, not even when I was young; not until you appeared; and I fell in love; and there was that wonderful and awful fusion of hope and despair. For the first time real, real hope, Elena; real, real belief. And yes, for the first time utter despair, utter desperation. Have you any idea at all of what I'm saying to you?

ELENA When you say you love me, Vanya, I feel no reaction at all; not even a curiosity about how *you* feel. That's the truth, Vanya. I feel nothing for you.

    She attempts to go. He blocks her.

VANYA You're throwing your life away, for God's sake! You know you are! What are you holding on to? What are you waiting for? What damned stupid convention is — ?

ELENA You're drunk, Vanya.

VANYA   I am not drunk.

ELENA   And aggressive.

VANYA   I am not aggressive.

ELENA   I'm going to bed. Where's the Doctor?

VANYA   Where's the Doctor? Why do you want to know where the Doctor is? The Doctor's in my room; sleeping in there tonight.

ELENA   You've been drinking again all day. Why do you do that, Vanya?

VANYA   Gives the illusion of life. Surely *you* understand that?

ELENA   You usen't drink so much and you usen't talk so much. You're becoming a boring old drunk.

He grabs her hand and kisses it.

VANYA   Beautiful — wonderful — astonishing woman —

ELENA   Leave me alone, will you?

She leaves. He is alone and almost calm.

VANYA   You first saw her when she was seventeen. Visiting Vera, sister Vera, who cried real tears. Ten years ago. Is that all? She was seventeen and you were thirty-seven. Why didn't you fall in love with her then and ask her to marry you? I don't know why you didn't, Vanya. I don't understand that. She would be your wife now, and the storm would have wakened her, and she would be frightened, and you would enfold her in your arms, and you would whisper to her, 'It's all right, my darling. Don't be afraid. You're safe. You're safe. I'm here, my darling. You're safe.' I often think I can feel her in my arms — I'm confused — I know I am — and it's not the wine — no, it's not the wine. But I *am* confused. Oh, yes. And I am old. And I don't understand why she doesn't understand what I'm saying to her. I don't understand that at all — (*Pours a drink*) Oh,

God, I'm a fool — such a fool. I used to be in awe of the Professor — I was — I was. Worked like a slave for him — we both did, Sonya and I. Squeezed every last drop we could out of the estate to send him money so that he could live in a style appropriate to his exalted position. Yes! Haggled for every farthing over vegetable oil and peas and cheese like a couple of greasy peasants; deprived ourselves of necessities just to keep him in luxury. We did — we did! Because we were proud of him and of his position and of his great scholarship. Because the life *he* was living — that was real life, life realized, life fulfilled, and it was our duty, we were pleased, we were honoured to service it. Yes! Yes! And now we know it was all a shell. A life-time of chicanery — spurious, fraudulent, empty. And that's what held us in awe. That's the life we serviced. Oh my God, what a fool I've been! What an utter fool!

Enter ASTROV, *he is drunk but articulate. His clothes are in disarray — he has been sleeping in them.* TELEGIN *follows with his guitar.*

ASTROV Play, Waffles. (*To* VANYA) I say that like the tzar, don't I? Play, vassal!

TELEGIN Everybody's asleep, Doctor.

ASTROV My people, they sleep too much.

TELEGIN He's in his stride! Fierce man when he's in his stride!

ASTROV (*Sings*) 'Come, let's to bed,'
says Sleepy-head.
'Tarry a while,'
says Slow.
Where are the women?

VANYA *shrugs.*

'Put on the pot,'
says Greedy Gut.
'I'll drink before I go.'
(*To* TELEGIN) Play!

While ASTROV *is singing the nursery rhyme above,*
TELEGIN *does an elaborate mime behind his back. It*
says: He's drunk. Just humour him. He'll waken the
house. Don't give him any drink.

TELEGIN Oh, he's a dangerous man! When the Doctor's in
top form, you do what you're bid!

TELEGIN *begins to play.*

ASTROV What time is it?

VANYA Late.

ASTROV Didn't I hear the voice of the dulcet Mrs
Serebryakov?

VANYA Gone to bed.

ASTROV With the athletic Alexander? Oh-ho! Magnificent
creature, isn't she? (*His eye falls on the array of*
medicines) For God's sake, just look at that!
Instant cures for gout from the four corners of
Holy Russia! Do you think he's really ill or just
looking for sympathy?

VANYA Ill.

ASTROV You don't feel sorry for him, do you? How could
you feel sorry for a man with a wife like that?

VANYA Don't you think you should — ?

ASTROV You envy him, Vanya.

VANYA Please, just —

ASTROV You're in love with her, aren't you?

VANYA I'm asking you —

ASTROV That's understandable. Oh-ho-ho-ho! Between
ourselves, Vanya, if you were to twist my arm,
you might even persuade me to join her in there
for an hour.

VANYA (*Evenly*) Careful, Astrov. You are over-stepping.

ASTROV Am I?

VANYA You are being crude. You are being offensive.

ASTROV Drunk, too. I know. Not that I offer that as extenuation. The crudeness is endemic. The offensiveness a kind of — robust flippancy — between friends. I usually get drunk like this once a month and when I do, I admit, I become a little arrogant. The drink empowers me in a miraculous way. Isn't that remarkable? When I'm drunk, my diagnoses are inspired. As for my surgery, the knife-work, at my very best — daring and exquisite.

TELEGIN (*Uncertainly*) Do you hear him! — Daring and exquisite. He's a comic, the Doctor. You're taking a hand at us, aren't you?

ASTROV When I'm drunk I devise sociological schemes that will transform all our lives. I'm not a freak! I'm a master philosopher who can change how we think and how we live. And from that eminence I look down on you all and I recognise you for what you really are — insects, microbes, nothings. What happened to the music?

TELEGIN We'll take a little rest, Doctor, will we? Don't want to waken the whole house, do we?

ASTROV Play, varlet!

TELEGIN I'm telling you — dangerous. He plays. He plays. What about a little German folk-song? Nothing to beat your German folk-song.

He strums softly.

ASTROV I need a drink, Vanya. (*Slightly blurred*) Sustenance for the arrogance. I'll say that again. (*Very distinctly*) Sustenance for the arrogance. I've a bottle of brandy in my room — well, your room — well, whoever's room — As Tchaikovsky here (*Telegin*) might put it, 'Claret's for boys, port's for men, but brandy's for heroes.'

SONYA *enters.*

As soon as it's light we'll drive to my place and —

He breaks off when he sees SONYA *staring at his dishevelled appearance.*

I'm afraid we're a little — we were discussing — Excuse me.

He dashes off. TELEGIN *is at his heels. As* TELEGIN *passes* SONYA *he flexes his arm muscles.*

TELEGIN All set for the hay in the morning. In prime form. If your hay's to be saved, Telegin's your man!

He exits.

SONYA (*With controlled anger*) Drinking with the Doctor again — why not? We all need to let go occasionally, don't we? That's understandable. I'm afraid the Doctor lets go too often for his own good, but then he's at least ten years younger than you.

VANYA No sermons, please.

SONYA And whatever about his drinking, he makes sure that *his* work never suffers.

VANYA Aren't illusions understandable?

SONYA Not when they take over your life. Look around you. The place is falling apart. The winter fuel hasn't even been brought in yet. The birds have destroyed all the fruit in the orchard. The hay can't be cut — it's rotting in the ground. And you have given up. Am I expected to do all the work myself? I really can't, Uncle Vanya. There are times when I'm so tired I can't even — (*Alarmed*) You're crying! Are you crying?

VANYA For God's sake, I'm not —

SONYA Yes, you are. What is it, Uncle Vanya!

VANYA It's just that — I caught a look in your face there

— and it was Vera, your mother, my beautiful Vera who cried real tears — (*He kisses her hands and her face again and again*) and suddenly I thought: if she could only see us now, what would she make of it all, if only she knew —

SONYA Knew what, Uncle?

VANYA Somehow it's all slowly crushing me and I don't know if I can go on. And it's not right somehow — something about it is all wrong, Sonya. Sorry —

He stumbles off. ASTROV, *now more sober than he was and now correctly dressed, enters.*

ASTROV Apologies. We have been a bit excessive. Did the music waken you?

SONYA I want to ask you a favour, Mikhail. Please don't drink with Uncle Vanya. It doesn't agree with him.

ASTROV We'll never drink together again.

SONYA Two glasses of wine after dinner is as much —

ASTROV That's settled. And I'm going.

SONYA Now? Wait till there's light.

ASTROV By the time the horses are saddled there'll be enough light.

SONYA And it's still pouring. What are you rushing off for?

ASTROV There's no point in sending me those urgent messages to come and see your father, Sonya. He ignores everything I say to him. Today he wouldn't even speak to me.

SONYA He's difficult, I know. He has been pampered all his life. At least you'll have something to eat before you go. Yes, do.

ASTROV All right. Why not?

She looks into the sideboard.

SONYA There's something a bit naughty about eating in the middle of the night, isn't there? Some cheese?

ASTROV Anything to soak up the alcohol. I haven't eaten all day. (*He lifts a bottle and pours himself a quick drink*) Ahhh! Better. Yes, a difficult man, your father. And old Vanya's getting odder by the day. And your grandmother's as close to eccentric as makes no difference. I don't think I'd survive a week in this house — without assistance (*glass*).

SONYA You don't need that, Mikhail.

ASTROV As for your step-mother — (*Examines bottle*) French. Good.

SONYA As for my step-mother?

ASTROV *St Justine*. Must remember that. Very good.

SONYA What were you going to say about Elena?

ASTROV I have a theory that people should be beautiful in *every* way — features, dress, speech, comportment, mind, soul — *completely* beautiful. In an ideal world. Outside our little cave. And on that checklist Elena scores very highly indeed. We delight in just looking at her beauty. We do — don't we?

SONYA Yes.

ASTROV But there is an element missing.

SONYA Is there?

ASTROV In bee-keeping language she's a drone. She has no responsibilities. She does no work. So that finally she accomplishes, she achieves, nothing. How can she? So she is not the complete, that wholly beautiful person — from the ideal world. Nothing clarifies the mind like a good Burgundy.

SONYA Are you complete?

ASTROV You mean do people delight in looking at me?

SONYA Mikhail!

ASTROV I'm like your Uncle Vanya in some ways: we're not sure what we expect from life but it disappoints us.

SONYA It does not!

ASTROV All the time.

SONYA I hear people say that and I do try to understand what it means but I can't. How can life — ?

ASTROV (*Testy, impatient*) The daily grind, dear — the day-to-day drudgery — that's what I mean. I'm not talking about 'existence', about 'being', for God's sake! I'm talking about rising in the morning and driving yourself through that grim routine of work and duty and then collapsing exhausted into bed. I'm talking about filthy hovels and smelling wounds and blankets that stink of urine. I'm talking about the noble Russian peasant; unwashed, uncivilised, ungrateful. And I'm talking about our 'educated' people around here with their trips to France and their powerful political friends in Petersburg and the books they must read and the recitals they can't possibly miss. As uncivilised in their own way and not all that clean either, who can barely bring themselves to speak to me unless they need me. 'Something a bit sinister about that Astrov fellow. Drinks too much! And refuses to eat meat! (*Whispers*) And he has this passion for young saplings! *Incroyable!*'

SONYA (*Laughs*) There must be somebody you like.

ASTROV Nanny. She reminds me of my old nanny. The embittered exterior always hides a sentimental core, doesn't it?

SONYA Your standards are too exacting, Mikhail; especially on yourself.

ASTROV *pours another drink and looks at the bottle again.*

ASTROV *St Justine* is very agreeable but vodka is more efficient.

SONYA And you don't need that.

ASTROV You know what my needs are?

SONYA *hesitates, then chooses her words carefully.*

SONYA I only know what I see, Mikhail. You aren't like

anybody else I know. You are a compassionate man and a genuinely good man. In your own way you are that 'beautiful' person. You are! And that (*Drink*) is destroying you. You are the one who says that people don't create — they only destroy what God has given us. You mustn't destroy the great, great gifts God has given you, Mikhail. You mustn't.

ASTROV You're so earnest!

SONYA Please, please don't.

He puts the bottle and glass aside.

ASTROV I'll never drink again.

SONYA Promise?

ASTROV A solemn vow.

They shake hands.

SONYA You *are* beautiful, you know. You must believe that.

ASTROV Absolutely. Apart from one weakness I'll confess only to you. I'm now so old and so coarsened by the drudgery of work that I haven't an emotion left in my body. Or is that a weakness? It must be, mustn't it? Anyhow, I feel nothing anymore. Yes, yes, I look at someone like Elena and there is a flicker of desire — naturally there is. That's not what I'm talking about. I'm talking about — I suppose I'm talking about emotions, instincts, deep human responses that are animate with life, instinct with passion. Just before Easter I operated on a man from Malitskoye. I was exhausted but I was cold sober. He died under the anaesthetic.

SONYA I know. You told me.

ASTROV Did I?

SONYA You've got to stop dwelling on that. (*Briskly*) So you haven't an emotion in your body? Right. A young woman looks you straight in the face and says straight out, 'I am in love with you'. What do you say to her?

ASTROV I say to her, 'My dear young woman, I am incapable of loving you or anybody else. And besides, my life is too full of — business.' And, I've got to go: tomorrow I've a list of calls the length of your arm. (*Shakes her hand*) I'll go out this way. Don't want to meet Vanya and break my solemn vow so soon.

He stops at the door.

The interesting thing about drones is —

SONYA Sorry?

ASTROV Bees! You've heard of bees? When their normal services aren't needed anymore, when the honey-flow comes to an end, the worker bees kill them off.

He goes.

SONYA Do they? Oh my God — 'You are that beautiful person' — that's what I said straight into his face! Oh my God, I should never have said that, should I? Yes, I should — it's true — it's true! And he revealed so little. Nothing! God knows what he really thinks. But for some reason I am happy. Are you? Yes, I am, I think I am, very happy. I love his vibrant voice. I love his calming eyes. I love his weary expression. And when he looks at me — Dear God, I would love to be beautiful. I would so love to be beautiful to him so that he could delight just in looking at me.

ELENA *enters.*

ELENA The storm is passing over, thank goodness. (*She opens the window*) The atmosphere is lighter

44

already. Where's the Doctor?

SONYA Gone.

ELENA What was that?

SONYA The Doctor's gone home.

ELENA goes to SONYA's side.

ELENA You have got to stop this sulking with me, Sonya. Please. Is there any reason in the world why we shouldn't be friends — is there?

SONYA I suppose not.

ELENA Please.

A moment's hesitation — then SONYA embraces her.

SONYA No reason in the world. I'm sorry. No more sulking. It's just that sometimes I —

ELENA Shhh.

SONYA I'm sorry.

ELENA The storm's away to the East.

SONYA Thank goodness. Is Father asleep?

ELENA He's back down in the drawing-room. (*She sees the sideboard open*) What's this?

SONYA Mikhail had some supper.

ELENA And wine!

SONYA A midnight orgy!

ELENA So let us drink to us — from the same glass.

SONYA Yes!

ELENA From his glass. (*Toasts*) To us — to real friendship — to an affectionate friendship.

SONYA kisses her.

SONYA I've wanted to do that for a long time and every time I —

ELENA Why are you crying?

SONYA I'm stupid, that's why. Stupid Sonya, that's what they called me at school.

ELENA And now you have me crying, too. Come on!

	This is silly. I do understand why you've been hostile to me, Sonya —
SONYA	Elena!
ELENA	All right; wary of me. You know you have. Because you always felt that I married your father — what do they say in novels? — for ignominious reasons. But I give you my word of honour, I married him because I loved him. I was mesmerised by the great scholar, the celebrated Professor. That's what I fell in love with. Of course it wasn't real love — what is real love? — But at the time it seemed very real to me. And since the day we were married you haven't stopped condemning me — all right, interrogating me — with those guarded eyes of yours.
SONYA	I haven't, have I? I'm sorry, Elena. No more interrogations.
ELENA	Do you believe me? About your father.
SONYA	Of course I believe you.
ELENA	We can't get on with our lives if we don't trust people, you know.
SONYA	And how are things now?
ELENA	Things?
SONYA	You and Father. Are you happy?
ELENA	No.
SONYA	You wish you were married to a younger man?
ELENA	Of course I do! You're such a goose, Sonya! (*She laughs*) No more interrogations, she says. Go on — next question.
SONYA	Do you like the Doctor?
ELENA	Yes.
SONYA	How much?
ELENA	A lot.
SONYA	So do I, Elena, so do I! Look at me — I have a big stupid smile on my face, haven't I? He's only just gone but his eyes, his voice, the way he moves — the whole aura of him — it's still altogether here. Feel it! The place is instinct with his passion!
ELENA	It's what?

SONYA What do you think of him? He has a magnetism,
hasn't he? He's — magnetic, isn't he? Oh God,
listen to me! What sort of an eejit am I? What do
you think of him?

ELENA I think he's —

SONYA He's so clever, isn't he? No, he's brilliant. And
he's a wonderful doctor. And he's expert at trees.
And you have no idea how much good he does
in all those miserable villages scores of miles
away. What do you think of him?

ELENA May I? I think he's a kind of genius —

SONYA He is — isn't he?

ELENA And I suppose a genius is someone who has a
vision and the self-confidence and the sheer
determination to pursue that vision. He sets out
to accomplish something extraordinary and
nothing will stop him.

SONYA Nothing in the world!

ELENA When he plants his trees he's already looking a
thousand years ahead and imagining the effect
they will have on future generations. I don't
know anybody else like that, do you? All right,
he drinks too much. So what are we asking of
him — that he takes two glasses of white wine
after dinner? That he lives the kind of measured
life the rest of us live? He's away outside our
conventions; far beyond them. And good luck
to him, I say; great, great, good luck. Look at
that radiant face! (*She kisses* SONYA) If anyone
deserves happiness, you do.

ELENA *moves away.* YEFIM *begins to sing again.*

In this life there are the people who lead and
those who stumble after them. I've always been
a stumbler: behind my husband; in my attempts
at a career in music; in all those silly romances
when I was young. A woman of absolutely no con-
sequence — ever. You are looking at a very, very

unhappy woman. And you're laughing at me.

SONYA No, no, I'm not. I just can't stop — I'm just so happy, Elena.

ELENA I am going to play the piano! One in the morning is the time to play the piano! I'll accompany Yefim!

SONYA Great idea. (*Hugs her*) You play — I'll dance! — I'll sing!

ELENA Wait a minute. Your father — he's awake and when he's off-colour, sometimes music annoys him. Go and ask him would he mind if I played something, would you?

SONYA Mind? Of course he won't mind! (*Embraces* ELENA) We'll flood the house with happiness, Elena!

SONYA *goes off.* ELENA *goes to the open window.*

ELENA Yefim?

YEFIM Yes, Ma'am?

ELENA I'm going to play the piano. I haven't played for ages and I am going to be just terrible. So I'm going to cry like a fool, Yefim.

YEFIM Yes, Ma'am.

SONYA *returns.*

ELENA Well?

SONYA He says no.

End of Act Two.

ACT THREE

*The drawing-room in the Serebryakov house. There are three doors —
one left, one centre, one right. It is early afternoon.*

ELENA *is walking around restlessly, dipping into a novel, discard-
ing it, picking it up again.* SONYA *is sitting on a couch.* VANYA *is
arranging chairs. He is a man close to break-down: his speech is rapid,
his manner either melancholy or exuberant — foreshadows of the
explosion that comes later.*

VANYA *surveys his work.*

VANYA That should do it. The distinguished Professor
will stand here and we will sit docilely there.
(*Looks at his watch*) Quarter to one. Fifteen min-
utes until he delivers his message to mankind.
What, pray, can the Great Sage have to tell us?
My curiosity is boundless. I doubt if I can contain
myself.

ELENA Probably some dreary business thing.

VANYA Business? — the Professor of Art? — *business?*

SONYA Uncle Vanya!

VANYA Sorry — sorry — sorry — sorry. Look at that
vision (*Elena*), would you? Such languor, such
languishing, such exquisite ennui. How *does* she
manage to keep on her feet?

ELENA How do you manage to keep up that endless
blathering?

VANYA It's miraculous!

ELENA Bored stiff, Vanya. Bored — bored — bored —
bored.

SONYA There's plenty to do if you wanted to, Elena.

ELENA Like what?

SONYA A lot of the old people in the village are sick with
'flu. Or you could teach the local children.

ELENA Me?

SONYA Or help run the estate. Before you and Father lived here, Uncle Vanya and I used to go to the market to sell our own flour. Didn't we?

VANYA (*Vaguely*) We did — didn't we?

ELENA Teaching snotty little brats? Looking after old, sick people? Are you serious, Sonya? You can't see me striding round the countryside in a sensible skirt and wellingtons, can you? It's only in 'improving' novels that people behave like that.

SONYA Isn't it natural to *want* to do things like that?

ELENA (*Totally puzzled*) Natural?

SONYA (*Embraces her*) A suggestion — only a suggestion. And your boredom has affected us all. Look at us. Uncle Vanya does nothing now but trail around behind you with his mouth open. I should be sweeping out the granary and I'm here to talk to you; a natural worker turned into a drone! And the Doctor who used to drop in maybe once a month — if we were lucky — now he's here every day. His patients, his trees, abandoned! Maybe you're a witch, Elena, are you?

VANYA No, a mermaid, a sea-nymph, our Amphitrite. So just for once be yourself and plunge into the wine-dark sea and give yourself to the mighty Poseidon and leave us all gasping on the shore — with our mouths open.

ELENA Why are you trying to hurt me, Vanya?

VANYA I'm not — I'm not — I'm sorry — that's the last thing in the world I'd want to do — I'm sorry — forgive me. (*Kisses her hand*) Am I forgiven?

ELENA Either hurting or grovelling or just being —

VANYA I've got a bunch of roses for you. Picked them for you this morning. Roses — autumn roses — beautiful, mournful, autumn roses.

He dashes off to get them.

SONYA Beautiful, mournful, autumn roses —

SONYA *and* ELENA *look out into the garden.*

ELENA September already. How are we going to get through the damned winter here? Where's the Doctor?

SONYA In Vanya's room, working on his maps. I must talk to you, Elena.

ELENA What about?

SONYA Oh, God, what about —

SONYA *suddenly embraces* ELENA *and rests her head on* ELENA*'s shoulder.*

ELENA Here — here — here — here — here — are you all right? What's all this, Sonya?

SONYA If I had been beautiful, Elena.

ELENA You have beautiful hair and your —

SONYA People always say to a plain-looking woman, 'You have beautiful hair; and such expressive eyes; and such a sweet nature.' I have loved him for over six years now, Elena. Love him more than I ever loved anybody. I hear his voice all day long. I feel his two hands enclosing mine. I keep gazing at the door in the hope that it will open and he will walk in. I keep running to you just so that I can talk about him. He's here every day now, every single day, and he doesn't look at me, doesn't even know I'm here. My heart is breaking, Elena. I ask God to give me strength just to carry on. I spent all of last night on my knees, asking God to give me strength, because whatever silly dignity and self-control I once had, they're all gone, Elena. I told Uncle Vanya yesterday, 'I love Mikhail Astrov' — said it straight out. I have no disguises left, Elena. I am almost throwing myself at him.

ELENA He knows, doesn't he?

SONYA Doesn't even see me.

ELENA I wouldn't believe that; he's a strange creature.

I'll tell you what: I'll talk to him.

SONYA Oh, no — !

ELENA I'll be very discreet; so subtle he won't even know I'm probing. The question is simple: he either loves you or he doesn't love you. Yes or No. You can't go on like this — not knowing — can you? If it's No, then he must stop coming here. It would be easier for you if you weren't to see him at all, wouldn't it? So. This is the moment. He has some stupid maps he's insisting on showing me. Tell him I'll look at them now. Here.

SONYA Whatever he says to you, you'll tell me, Elena — *everything* he says?

ELENA You'll hear the whole truth — everything he says — every syllable.

SONYA (*Dreamily*) Tell him you'll look at them now. Here. (*She stops at the door*) I don't want to know the truth, Elena. Don't tell me the truth. There's still a possibility of hope when you don't know the truth, isn't there?

ELENA There's still what?

SONYA Nothing — sorry — nothing —

She goes off.

ELENA People shouldn't burden you with their secrets when there's nothing you can do about them. Because he's not in love with her — that's obvious to everybody but her. Of course that doesn't mean that he couldn't marry her. She has a sweet nature and she'd be an excellent wife for a country doctor who's not exactly a boy anymore. Because she's bright and she's considerate and she's — diligent, that's the word — as if any of that matters in the slightest — And why wouldn't she be restless in this damned — quagmire? You know exactly how she feels, don't you? Oh, indeed you do: rising, talking, eating, sleeping; the thrilling pattern of our lives day in, day out, seven days a week. So that picking gooseberries is an occasion. A new roof on this granary is an event. The arrival of the thresher — good God, that is a Greek drama! And then he appears — aloof — engaged — diffident — arrogant. And of course she's spellbound. In this setting he's almost exotic, isn't he? So that when he appears the day suddenly has that little frisson, that whiff of unease, that scent of danger, doesn't it? And listening to you, Elena, I suspect you're not altogether immune yourself. Why are you smiling? Vanya says you have mermaid blood in your veins, doesn't he? So why not take that plunge into the wine-dark sea? Why not? And in that defiant plunge escape forever from this damned prison and all the prisoners in it? Why not indeed? — Because you're too cowardly and too timid. Even though you know in your heart why he comes here every day now, don't you? Oh, yes, you know very well. So really you should be asking Sonya to forgive you, shouldn't you?

ASTROV *enters briskly with his maps and charts up to his chin. As he usually is with* ELENA, *he is a little defensive.*

ASTROV Ah! There you are. Up to my eyes — as usual.
ELENA You said you'd show me what you're working at.
ASTROV Did I?
ELENA Are you going to show me?
ASTROV Do you want to see it?
ELENA Yes!
ASTROV It won't bore you?
ELENA Why should it bore me?
ASTROV You're a city woman, aren't you? — Petersburg? — College of Music — right?
ELENA Yes.
ASTROV This wouldn't interest you then. Rustic stuff.

Bumpkin stuff.

ELENA I know a lot about 'rustic stuff'. I *am* interested, Mikhail.

ASTROV I've set up my own work-table here now; in Vanya's quarters. When I'm completely exhausted I turn the key in the surgery and run over here and amuse myself for a few hours. We must be a funny-looking trio: Vanya and Sonya clicking away on their counting-frame and me messing with my maps and my paints. You should look in on us: big fire — nobody speaking — crickets chirping on the hearth. Very essence of rural contentment — Right. The Lecture — since you insist. I've made three maps. Map One. Move a little closer.

ELENA I'm fine here.

ASTROV Our district as it was fifty years ago. The dark green and light green are trees, forestation. As you can see, half the area was wooded. Those red patches through the green are elk and wild goat. This lake — can you see it?

ELENA Yes.

ASTROV That was a breeding-ground for swans and geese and wild duck; there was a 'power' of them, as the locals say. Villages here and here and here. Watermills. Two small monasteries, hermitages, really. And these blue areas — they're all over the place — those were cattle and horses. Herds of them. Fifty years ago every farm had two, maybe three, horses. Are you awake?

ELENA Mikhail!

ASTROV Facetious. Map Two. The same district twenty-five years later. The dark green and light green forests have now shrunken to a third. There are still a few elk but the wild goats have disappeared. Fewer blue and green areas: the horses are already on the way out. So the process of decline is well advanced. Map Three. I'm only an amateur cartographer. They're a bit crude.

ELENA They're very pretty.

ASTROV (*Tartly*) Pretty? I hadn't thought of them as pretty. Our district as it is today. Still the odd patch of green — that I'm defending with my life. There are fewer of them and they're not as dense. But the elks have vanished. And the wild goats. And the swans. And the wild duck. Even the lake has dried up. The outlying villages have disappeared. And the watermills. And the monasteries. So the decline has been rapid and relentless. And if some fool decides in twenty-five years' time to make Map Four, it will be a picture of total desolation. A blank grey sheet, maybe. Not at all pretty. Can this devastation be arrested? Oh, no, we're told! It's inevitable. The old must make way for the new. The old has given way all right — that's obvious. But where is the new? Where are the roads, the railways, the schools, the hospitals, the factories that would bring some vigour, some health to the district? I don't see them. I still see the swamps and the mosquitoes and the disease and the poverty. They're all still abundantly with us. So is it surprising that the peasants have given up hope? Of course they are backward and ignorant and lazy and stubborn because this is all they have ever known — this squalor, this degradation, this hopelessness. Is it any wonder they have no sense of preservation? If your child is sick or cold or hungry, are you going to grab at anything that will fill its stomach and keep it warm *now*? Or are you going to scruple over some delicate balance in nature, some ecological nicety? To hell with tomorrow — you're going to grab today, aren't you? And if that means some physical imbalance, some biological discord in the future — too damned bad! And I'm over-heating. And you are bored.

ELENA Not at all.

ASTROV 'Course you are. End of tedious lecture. (*Busies*

himself gathering up his maps)

ELENA I am not bored, Mikhail. It's just that there is so much to take in and it's all so —

ASTROV Dull?

ELENA — so disturbing that it's hard to —

ASTROV Doesn't matter. Private obsession.

ELENA And there's something else I'm anxious about — something I'd like to talk to you about.

ASTROV (*Ironically*) The flora and fauna! You thought I forgot them!

ELENA Something I want to ask you — if you would just —

ASTROV They're clearly marked on Map One but almost wiped out in Map Three.

ELENA I want to talk to you about Sonya, Mikhail.

ASTROV Who?

ELENA My step-daughter, Sonya.

ASTROV I *know* she's your —

ELENA Do you like her?

ASTROV I like Sonya; yes.

ELENA Do you like her a lot?

ASTROV I admire Sonya.

ELENA Does she attract you as a woman?

ASTROV No. Am I in the witness-box?

ELENA She's in love with you.

ASTROV Elena —

ELENA Yes, she is. Haven't you noticed? And she's utterly miserable because you don't love her — obviously.

ASTROV I am very fond of Sonya; and I think she will —

ELENA So the kindest thing you could do — since you are so fond of her — the most considerate thing would be to stop coming here altogether.

ASTROV Stop — ?

ELENA I can't tell you how unhappy she is.

ASTROV So I must — ?

ELENA She loves you, Mikhail. She's mad about you. And you don't love her. There's nothing more to say. No more questions. And now I'm blushing. I wouldn't have made a good barrister, would I?

ASTROV Oh God — I can't believe that she — the poor child. But of course if she's as unhappy as you say — And what's your role in all this?

ELENA Role?

ASTROV Who gave you this brief?

ELENA What brief?

ASTROV Whose side are you on here, Elena?

He looks closely into her face and wags his finger at her.

Elena's side, of course. You're a sly little pussy-cat, aren't you?

ELENA I don't know what that means.

ASTROV (*Laughs*) Indeed you do. So Sonya is unhappy. So Sonya is utterly miserable. But why interrogate me? Surely not to discover why I come here — because you know the answer to that.

ELENA I do?

ASTROV Come on, Elena.

ELENA How should I know why —

ASTROV Stop fluttering those innocent eyes at me. Neither of us is a novice at this game. I come here every day to see you, my beautiful young falcon —

ELENA Mikhail, I —

ASTROV You don't like 'falcon'? You're right. Too free. Too ethereal. Because you're solidly of the earth, aren't you? Grounded and guarded. What about a weasel, smooth and silky and hungry for victims? Yes, I throw everything up and come panting over here just to gaze at you. You know I do. And you love it! God, how you love to have me here on my knees! So forget your devious questions and your bogus concern for Sonya. I confess! Take me! Devour me!

ELENA You are out of your mind, Mikhail.

ASTROV I must be, mustn't I?

57

ELENA And I don't know what sort of woman you think I am. But I can tell you, you have read me wrongly, altogether wrongly.

She tries to leave. He blocks her way.

ASTROV I'll leave today. I won't come back. (*He grabs her hand*) But we've got to meet. Where can I see you? (*Looks around*) Before someone comes in. Tell me quickly — where? — where? God, you are absolutely, utterly beautiful! I want to kiss your hair and your neck and your arms and your hands and —

ELENA Mikhail, I swear to God —

ASTROV Don't speak — don't utter a word. Just let me hold you and kiss you and —

ELENA Stop it, Mikhail! Stop — stop — stop —

ASTROV When will you meet me? Tomorrow? Where — where? I'm not giving up. It is going to happen. Just tell me where. Because it is going to happen — you know it is.

He kisses her. And at that moment VANYA *enters with his roses and stops in the doorway. Neither* ELENA *nor* ASTROV *sees him.*

ELENA Oh, God, Mikhail — this is awful — (*She embraces him quickly*) Now go! Please go! Now!

ASTROV The plantation — tomorrow — two o'clock. You'll be there — you want to be there — don't you?

ELENA *now sees* VANYA. *She breaks away from* ASTROV *and goes to the window.*

ELENA Oh my God — oh, Vanya — Oh God —

VANYA *leaves the roses on a chair and mops his face and neck with his handkerchief.*

VANYA It's all right — there they are (*roses*) — not to worry — it's all right — fine —

ASTROV (*With bravado*) Well timed, Vanya: just missed my lecture. The Decline and Fall of the Dostrovsky District. I do it without notes now; absolutely; and I believe with some theatricality. I try to fake some passion when I come to the Fall. (*Gathers his maps*) The days *are* getting shorter, aren't they? Afraid the summer's over.

He exits quickly. ELENA *goes to* VANYA.

ELENA Alexander and I have got to leave here today, Vanya! You've got to see that that happens! Help me, Vanya. I need your help.

VANYA What's that? — Oh, yes — 'Absolutely', as he says — I saw what was happening, Elena. I stumbled in on it all, didn't I? — Yes, I'm afraid —

Voices off.

ELENA Listen to me! We've got to leave! Today! Now! Help me, Vanya.

Enter SEREBRYAKOV, TELEGIN, SONYA *and* MARINA.

SEREBRYAKOV One o'clock on the dot and here we are.

TELEGIN The thing about your climate is this, Professor: he is wrought out of cunning. Put on light clothes and he hits you with a storm — and suddenly you're frozen. Put on heavy clothes and he hits you with a heat-wave — and suddenly you're lashing. We haven't got his measure yet and that's why he's laughing at us.

SEREBRYAKOV (*Totally puzzled*) Is he?

TELEGIN Splitting his sides. But your German has his measure. Your German fights him with the right clothes, the right shoes, the right hats. In fact your German has him damn near on his knees.

SEREBRYAKOV Splendid! Are we all assembled? Where's my wife?

ELENA I'm here.

SEREBRYAKOV Ah. And my mother-in-law? (*To* SONYA — *who does not hear him*) Tell your grandmother we're waiting for her. Everyone found a seat? Over here, Nanny, please. Excellent.

SONYA (*To* ELENA) What did he say?

ELENA Tell you later.

SONYA Tell me now. You're as white as a sheet, Elena. He's never coming back again — isn't that it? That's what he said — isn't it?

ELENA *nods 'yes'.*

SONYA Knew it all along — Oh, God, Elena —

SEREBRYAKOV Can't get a breath in this damned room. Would somebody please open that window?

TELEGIN *opens the window.*

Thank you. Are we all here? Nanny's missing.

MARINA Am I?

SEREBRYAKOV Didn't see you, Nanny. My mistake. A seat here, Telegin. Elena — over here.

TELEGIN *sits and fans himself.*

TELEGIN Would anyone object if I took off my jacket?

SEREBRYAKOV And now at last —

TELEGIN Between seasons.

SEREBRYAKOV — I think we're ready to open the meeting.

VANYA I don't think I'm needed. So if you don't mind, I'll —

SEREBRYAKOV Of course you're needed, Vanya. You're the most needed person here.

VANYA Why?

SEREBRYAKOV Take a seat, please.

VANYA What am I needed for?

SEREBRYAKOV In due course. And not an occasion for belligerence, Vanya.

VANYA Belligerence?

SEREBRYAKOV In character of course but out of place today. Who's still missing? Mother-in-law. Anybody seen — ?

MARIA *enters with her books and pamphlets.*

MARIA A protest meeting! Excellent!

SEREBRYAKOV Just sit down, Maman.

MARIA I'm voting No. Do you hear me?

SEREBRYAKOV I hear you.

MARIA With the Nays.

SEREBRYAKOV Yes.

MARIA No.

SEREBRYAKOV Yes. We're all here. Let's begin then. I'll be as concise as possible. I have asked you to join me here this afternoon because I seek your good counsel. As you know, I am a scholar and only a scholar. My life has been lived exclusively in the realm of the mind; so that the world of commerce — as some would have it, the 'real world' — I'm afraid I'm foreign to it and it to me. So I'm looking to you, Vanya, and to you, Telegin, Sonya, mother-in-law —

MARIA No!

SEREBRYAKOV — to you all, all my close friends, for wise guidance. The situation is this. I am an old man. I am an ill man. And now in the winter of my days, I want to settle my affairs for my own peace of mind and for the sake of my young wife and my unmarried daughter. (*Pause*) We cannot go on living in the country. Country life is inimical to the life of the intellect. We have got to go back to the city, to the sharp, swift current of ideas. Which brings us to the very nub of the problem: money. Can we afford it? Not, I'm afraid, on the income this estate generates. So what can be done? I know what your immediate and typically generous response will be. 'Let's sell the forests!', you will say to me. 'That will realise the money you need just now!' And indeed it would, thank you kindly. But as a one-off solution. Then what? No, no, we must all of us put our wise heads together and devise a scheme that guarantees an adequate income and a regular income. And what occurred to me was this — and please, please be tolerant of my incursion into territories, that 'real world', I know nothing about, that frightens me in fact. What occurred to me was this. I propose — formally — that we sell the estate and invest eighty-five per cent of the capital in government securities. They yield a minimum of four per cent in the present climate.

TELEGIN In the present climate — he's right!

SEREBRYAKOV With the balance of that capital, the outstanding fifteen per cent, I propose buying a villa somewhere in the Petersburg area. Now — how does that appeal to you all?

Silence.

TELEGIN Nice soft breeze.

VANYA I think I must have missed something here. Say that again, Alexander, would you?

SEREBRYAKOV The money would be invested in government stocks and the balance would purchase a villa somewhere —

VANYA No, no, not the villa bit — before that — before that — what did you say?

SEREBRYAKOV I propose selling the estate.

VANYA This estate?

SEREBRYAKOV Is there another estate I don't know of? (*Laughs*) Yes, Vanya, this estate.

VANYA Ah. You propose selling this estate. I see. And Mother — and Sonya — and me — what will become of us?

SEREBRYAKOV That is step two, Vanya. Let's keep focussed on the first stage.

VANYA I'm being stupid — of course I am; and thick-skulled and obtuse and imbecilic and asinine and idiotic and doltish and everything else you can think of. Because I always believed — I can't be wrong about this, can I? — I always *knew* that my father bought this estate as a dowry for my sister, Vera; and when Vera died, it passed on to her daughter, Sonya. But maybe I'm crazy. Could I have gone a bit crazy?

SEREBRYAKOV The estate *is* Sonya's.

VANYA And you propose to — ?

SEREBRYAKOV I propose that it be put up for sale —

VANYA But if the estate is not — ?

SEREBRYAKOV — with her approval and in her own best interests.

VANYA In her own best — ? Ah! One of us is crazy. One of us must be crazy!

MARIA Don't interrupt Alexander, Vanya. He knows much better than you or I what is right and what is wrong.

VANYA I need a drink of something. (*Drinks*) D'you know, that is really good water. (*To* SONYA) You were so right to have that upper well cleaned. And the sun is coming out! I must prune that rose bed behind the saddle room. And I love that shirt, Telegin.

TELEGIN Do you? Cotton.

VANYA Is it really?

TELEGIN German cotton.

VANYA Never! German?

TELEGIN Just perfect. The niece sent it from Hamburg.

VANYA Good God! (*To* ALL) His niece sent him a cotton shirt all the way from Hamburg!

SEREBRYAKOV No need to get worked up, Vanya. My proposal is no more than a proposal. If you all decide against it, we'll forget it.

TELEGIN If I may say something, Professor, with your per-

mission. I do happen to know a little about the
history of this estate because —

VANYA He knows all about it. Father bought it from his
uncle. That is why Telegin lives here as our guest.

TELEGIN Ever since my fortunes took a little dip.

VANYA The price was ninety-five thousand roubles.

TELEGIN As fortunes do.

VANYA Father paid seventy thousand —

TELEGIN In cash.

VANYA — and got a bank loan for the balance. He could
never have afforded it if I hadn't signed over my
share of the inheritance in favour of my sister,
my sister Vera who shed real tears; and that I did
with all my heart.

TELEGIN My fortunes didn't take a little dip until much
later.

VANYA As well as that —

MARIA Vanya, you —

VANYA Keep quiet! As well as that I worked like an ox
for ten years until the bank loan was paid off —

SEREBRYAKOV Why did I ever start this?

VANYA — with the result that the estate is now free of
debt and in good shape and all because I worked
myself to the bone and now in my old age I'm to
be kicked out on the roadside. Wonderful!

SEREBRYAKOV Nobody is going to kick you —

VANYA For twenty-five years I've run this place more
faithfully than any manager; and for twenty-five
years money was sent to him every month; and
for twenty-five years I earned the same princely
salary, five hundred roubles. Never one rouble
more. Never an offer of one rouble more. For
twenty-five years never even a Thank You, for
God's sake!

SEREBRYAKOV I was never a practical man — unlike you. Had
you helped yourself to more money, I wouldn't
have noticed.

VANYA Why didn't I steal? You're mocking me now
because I didn't steal from you? In all justice I

should have, shouldn't I? And I wouldn't be the pauper I am now.

MARIA He wouldn't be what? What did he say?

TELEGIN (*Goes to* VANYA) Easy, Vanya. Not worth getting worked up about. Don't want the happy domestic climate to take a little dip, do we?

VANYA Shut up, Telegin! (*To* SEREBRYAKOV) For twenty-five years we've been buried here like moles, Mother and Sonya and I, working for you, but as importantly, more importantly, *thinking* of you all the time.

TELEGIN Easy.

SEREBRYAKOV Is this leading us anywhere?

VANYA Because we believed that that man was some kind of superior being. Incredible but absolutely true! And everything he said, everything he wrote, we believed, we knew that it was an utterance of genius; and our little moles' eyes gleamed with wonder and reverence and unqualified delight.

SEREBRYAKOV This is becoming tedious.

VANYA I know now we were just a little mistaken, don't I? I know now that the work is worthless and the career fraudulent and the man himself one plump charlatan. For twenty-five years you made fools of us all.

SEREBRYAKOV That will do, Vanya.

ELENA You're being hurtful, Vanya. You're being hysterical.

VANYA I offered the best years of my life to him and they were devoured by his vanity and his pomposity and then spat out at my feet.

ELENA Vanya, stop it!

VANYA That man is my enemy.

TELEGIN I really can't take — the atmosphere is suffocating me — pardon me —

He exits quickly.

SEREBRYAKOV I'm weary of your rant, little man. If the damned
estate is yours, keep it. I will not be insulted by a
nonentity.

ELENA For God's sake — please — please! (*Shouts*) I
can't stand this any longer!

VANYA *goes to his mother. He speaks very softly.*

VANYA I was never a wild man, a dissolute man, not
even in my youth, was I, Mother? I think I was
disciplined, wasn't I? And courageous and intel-
ligent enough, too, wasn't I? If I had had a
normal life, God knows what I might have
become. Maybe your son would have been a
Schopenhauer, Mother — a Dostoyevsky maybe!
I am desperate, Mother. You can see that, can't
you? I am so desperate. I think maybe I'm losing
my reason.

MARIA Just do whatever Alexander proposes.

SONYA *kneels at* MARINA's *feet and hugs her knees.*

SONYA Nanny — Nanny — Oh, God, Nanny —

MARINA Shhhhh.

VANYA I'm sorry I can't do that, Mother. But something
must be done — yes, something must be done.
(*To* SEREBRYAKOV) And I am not a nonentity. Oh, no.

He exits through the middle door. MARIA *goes with
him. As she exits:*

MARIA I'll talk to him. He's a little drunk.

SEREBRYAKOV A little drunk? — That's good! The man's de-
ranged! Either he moves out to one of the
cottages or I will; but I will not spend another
night under this roof with that maniac!

ELENA We're leaving altogether, Alexander. We're going
today! We're going now!

SEREBRYAKOV Driven out by that madman? Certainly not!

SONYA (*On verge of tears*) Please try to be a little understanding, Father. Uncle Vanya and I are very
unhappy. You can see that, can't you? Remember
when I was a child? You must remember Uncle
Vanya and Grandma sitting up night after night,
translating articles from foreign languages for
you and writing out copies of your lectures and
reading through journals and papers that might
interest you. *I* remember that; night after night.
And all through the years Vanya and I have
worked as hard as we could so that we could
support you. It was all for you. I know this
sounds as if I'm saying — weren't we wonderful? That's not what I'm saying at all. What I'm
asking of you is just to look at us and see how
unhappy we are and maybe try to understand
why we are so unhappy. All you have to do is
look at us, Father.

ELENA Go and talk to him. He doesn't know what he's
saying. Just calm him down. Please.

SEREBRYAKOV All right — all right! I'll talk to him. The man has
wounded me deeply and permanently — you all
witnessed that. But he *is* hysterical — if that's an
excuse.

ELENA Don't mention the estate at all. And tell him
we're leaving today — now.

ELENA *and* SEREBRYAKOV *go out through the middle
door.* SONYA *goes back to* NANNY *and holds her.*

SONYA What's going to become of us all, Nanny?

MARINA Everything's going to be fine, my darling.
Believe me. I'm a wise old woman, amn't I? And
they're all geese. They cackle and they cackle and
finally they stop. That's just how geese behave.

SONYA I do believe you.

MARINA You're shivering. (*Hugs her*) There — there —
there — my little orphan. You take these things
too much to heart. And they're not all that

important. In the eyes of God they're probably not important at all.

A pistol shot off. ELENA *screams.*

Oh my God — !
SONYA What — what — what — ?

SEREBRYAKOV *staggers on. He is terrified.*

SEREBRYAKOV Stop him! He's gone mad! For God's sake —

ELENA *and* VANYA *appear in the doorway. They are struggling. She is trying to wrest the gun from him.*

ELENA Give it to me, Vanya!
VANYA No — no —
ELENA I'm telling you — give it to me — now!
VANYA Let me go! Take your hands off me! (*He breaks free*) Where is he? He's hiding from me! Ah, there he is! (*He fires*) Did I get him? Did I miss? Oh for God's sake, how could I miss again —

He sinks to the ground and bangs the revolver on the floor.

ELENA I must get away from this place. Take me away — kill me — but I can't stay here any longer — I can't — I can't —
VANYA What happened? — What am I doing — what have I done?
SONYA Oh Nanny, Nanny, Nanny, Nanny, Nanny —

End of Act Three.

ACT FOUR

Vanya's room which serves as his bedroom and as the office of the estate. A door left leads to the main house. A door right opens on to the hall.

Close to the window a large table with account books and various papers. A bureau. Some bookcases. A large set of scales.

A smaller table for Astrov. On it are his paints and drawing materials. Beside this smaller table a large portfolio. A cage containing a starling. On the wall hangs a big map of Africa, very out of place in these surroundings. A large sofa covered in oilcloth.

Close to the door right a mat for the peasants to wipe their feet.

It is late evening of the same day as Act Three. The place is very still.

TELEGIN *and* MARINA *are facing each other, winding wool.*
TELEGIN *is agitated.*

TELEGIN Listen! There's the carriage coming round to the front. They must be about to leave.

MARINA Move back.

TELEGIN Hurry up, will you? We're going to miss them.

MARINA We're going to miss nothing.

TELEGIN Far too late to be setting out. It will be midnight by the time they get to Kharkov.

MARINA Where?

TELEGIN You know — Kharkov; where they're going to.

MARINA Where's Kharkov?

TELEGIN How would I know? They're right to be getting away from here though. Did you hear her? — Elena. Hysterical. 'I've got to get away from this house! Anywhere! I won't spend another hour in this place!' Did you hear her?

MARINA (*Sharply*) Indeed I did.

TELEGIN Couldn't even take time to pack all their stuff. The rest will have to be sent on to them.

69

MARINA Disgraceful, that's what it was! Shouting and crying and shooting their guns! I never thought I'd see a scene like it in this house.

TELEGIN A little dip all right.

MARINA A *little* dip? Shameful! The sooner we get back to our old routine the better: breakfast at eight; dinner at one; and tea at seven. That was how a Christian family used to behave.

TELEGIN You're right, Marina.

MARINA At least a family that called itself Christian. Hold it (*wool*) a bit tighter.

TELEGIN I was walking through the village this morning; and old Boris was standing at the door of his shop; and just as I had passed him —

MARINA I'll take that end (*of wool*). Sorry?

TELEGIN Doesn't matter.

MARINA Juat as you had passed him — ?

TELEGIN Just as I had passed him he shouted after me; 'There goes Telegin, the sponger. Still living on hand-outs, Telegin?' There were a lot of people around. I was a bit hurt, Marina — you know. Just a little bit hurt.

MARINA Always a coarse creature, that Boris.

TELEGIN Suppose so.

MARINA And since his wife left him, more bitter than ever.

TELEGIN I'd forgotten that.

MARINA And even though we all work as hard as we can, in a way we all depend on God's hand-outs, don't we? Nobody pays the slightest attention to Boris anymore. Where's Sonya?

TELEGIN In the garden with the Doctor. Searching for Vanya. Afraid he might do some harm to himself.

MARINA Where's his revolver?

TELEGIN (*Whispers*) I have it.

MARINA You have not!

TELEGIN Hidden in the cellar.

MARINA Clever Ilya Telegin! Good for you!

VANYA *enters.* ASTROV *is immediately behind him,*

obviously following him.

VANYA Please stop following me, Doctor. (*To* MARINA *and* TELEGIN) And would you both mind conducting your business somewhere else? I would like to have my room to myself, if I may.

TELEGIN We're off. As Hans used to say to me (*In German accent*), 'You are in our way, Waffles. Please depart us.'

VANYA What is that man talking about?

MARINA (*To* VANYA) Quack — quack — quack — quack.

She gathers her belongings and she and TELEGIN *leave.*

VANYA And that is unnecessary, Nanny. (*To* ASTROV) And I'd ask you to go, too, if you wouldn't mind.

ASTROV (*Sits*) Sorry.

VANYA I will not be kept under surveillance as if I were somehow — a menace.

ASTROV I will go when you have returned what you took from me.

VANYA I took nothing from you.

ASTROV Don't be so childish. Either you hand it over voluntarily or we will tie you up and search you. Take your pick, Vanya. I want to get away, too.

VANYA Twice I fired at him and twice I missed him! How could I have missed him *twice*? It's unforgivable — I know it is.

ASTROV Why not turn it on yourself next time?

VANYA There's a bizarre logic at work here and I don't understand it. I've just tried to murder somebody but nobody even thinks of sending for the police. Why is that? Clearly because they must think I am not a criminal but just mad. Fine. So I am mad. But what about those charlatans who pose as intellectuals and make fools of us all? Are they mad — or criminals? And what about those women who marry those old charlatans and openly and brazenly deceive them? Aren't they criminals? The logic is bizarre, Astrov. It's a stupid logic. I saw you holding her in your arms.

ASTROV So you did.

VANYA I saw you kissing her, Astrov.

ASTROV That really nudged you over the top, didn't it?

VANYA You are a very cruel man. A society that produces people like you must be a very disturbed society.

ASTROV Don't be childish, Vanya.

VANYA Why not? I'm mad, amn't I? Aren't mad people entitled to be whatever they choose to be? Aren't they? — Aren't they?

ASTROV That's schoolboy stuff and it's just tedious. You're nothing as grand as mad, Vanya. Just a fool; a silly, old fool. I used to think that people like you were abnormal in some way. They're not. The world is populated with people like you — God help us.

VANYA I am so ashamed of myself; so immersed in self-contempt that my whole being is infected with it. If it were just a pain, I could handle it. Pain can be measured, can be faced up to. But this malign ghost — it's slowly killing me. Have you a cure for self-contempt?

ASTROV No.

VANYA I'm forty-seven. I suppose I could live until I'm sixty, couldn't I? Oh, dear God, no! Another thirteen years of this? You're a doctor. You must know what I'm talking about. Now and then the blackness fissures; very occasionally; but it happens — it happens; and a possibility of hope appears; and I think to myself, 'Imagine if the past was completely erased and it was possible — oh my God — it was possible to begin all over again!' Imagine the liberation, the ecstasy, of that, Astrov! To have another attempt at it all!

ASTROV Self-delusion.

VANYA Not a real hope — not even an expectation — just the possibility that —

ASTROV Self-indulgence. We live without hope, you and I.

VANYA Nobody can —

ASTROV (*Angrily*) Oh, shut up, Vanya! 'Not real hope — not even an expectation.' Face up to what *is* man. The life we lead is without hope. Face that. The life we lead is futile. Face that. Maybe future generations will discover a way of living that is full and fulfilling — and with no self-delusions. Good luck to them! As for us — ! (*Laughs*) There must be a positive side, a dip up, as Telegin puts it. Yes, there is. We have lived out our days in a mean-spirited society but to our eternal credit we have held on to an *idea* of other possibilities, of better things. Aren't we magnificent?

VANYA You're mocking me.

ASTROV Absolutely. And give me back what you stole from me.

VANYA I stole nothing from you.

ASTROV A bottle of morphine from my case. If you're hell-bent on doing yourself in, go out to the forest and blow your head off there. But it's damned thoughtless of you to use my morphine. People will assume I *gave* it to you, won't they? I'm happy to do a post-mortem on a shooting victim. But on a man who overdosed on *my* morphine? That's being selfish, Vanya.

SONYA *enters.*

VANYA Come to see the genial GP? Here he is — at his most sympathetic.

ASTROV (*To* SONYA) He has stolen a bottle of morphine from my case and he won't give it back. Tell him he's being stupid. Now, please. I've got to go.

SONYA Give it back to him, Uncle Vanya. You don't want to frighten us all, do you? (*She kneels beside him*) You're unhappy. I know that. Maybe I'm just as unhappy. But I'm not going to give up. I'm going to endure and I'll go on enduring until my life

comes to an end. So will you, sweet Uncle Vanya.
Together we will endure. All we need is patience.
(*She kisses his hands*) Now give him his morphine.
For my sake.

VANYA takes the bottle from his desk drawer and gives it to SONYA.

VANYA You give it to him.

She gives the bottle to ASTROV who puts it in his case.

ASTROV Silly bit of self-dramatisation, wasn't it?
SONYA Was it?
VANYA (*At his desk*) We must begin working again.
Immediately. If we don't begin immediately it
may be too late.
SONYA The moment the others leave. Nothing will stop
us then. (*She moves around the bundle of papers on
the desk*) Look — chaos! But we will make a start
tonight, Uncle Vanya. A first step.
ASTROV Fine. I can leave now.

ELENA enters.

ELENA We're about to go. (*To VANYA*) Alexander wants to
say something to you, Vanya.
VANYA 'My husband'.
ELENA Speak to him before we go, will you?
SONYA Yes, he will. (*Takes VANYA by the arm*) Come on,
Uncle Vanya. You and Father must make it up.
God knows when you'll see him again.

She leads VANYA off.

ELENA So — we're off.

She holds out her hand to ASTROV. He takes it.

ASTROV Just this minute?

ELENA Just this minute. The horses are round at the front.

ASTROV In that case — goodbye.

ELENA You promised me this afternoon you'd go away and stay away. You *will* do that?

ASTROV Promise. I'm leaving now, too. You gave yourself a bit of a fright, you know.

ELENA A fright?

ASTROV This afternoon. Meeting me in the plantation — will I — won't I? Oh, yes. Touch and go, wasn't it?

ELENA Was it?

ASTROV You can't leave now. Think up some excuse and tomorrow afternoon we'll —

ELENA We're going, Mikhail. And because we're going, I can see things more clearly. (*He drops her hand*) I still think you read me wrongly; because if I gave you the impression or if you got the impression —

ASTROV Chook — chook — chook — chook. I'll miss Nanny. I think I love Nanny. Where are you going to? Kharkov? God, Kharkov Of All Places! You know what your problem is, Elena? You have nothing to do, nothing to exercise your mind, absolutely no purpose to your existence; so that one of these days you are going to be ambushed by a great passion and you are going to abandon yourself totally to it — for a short time. Yes. Inevitable. But in Kharkov Of All Places! Have you no discrimination? What's wrong with here? Forests — lakes — gardens — elegant decay (*the house*) — the atmosphere of sad optimism — *the plantation*, Elena!

ELENA You drive me mad —

ASTROV Do I?

ELENA — because you try so hard to appear just cynical and in fact you are a complicated man.

ASTROV Saintly, according to Telegin.

75

ELENA And that's how I'll remember you. And since we won't meet again — yes, I do find you attractive, very attractive. Can we shake hands?

ASTROV Let's be daredevils. (*He takes her hand again and holds it*) And in fact you are a very complicated woman; but with an elusive thing I can't quite pin down. Here we were, beavering away, full of industry and dedication and high purpose; and suddenly you and your husband appear; and suddenly — suddenly — the beehive comes to a stand-still; and for the whole summer we do nothing but minister to your guiles and to his gout. My practice is forgotten; the damned peasants graze their animals in my newly-planted woods; and I stand here, gazing at you!

ELENA Mikhail!

ASTROV You have destroyed thousands of acres of saplings. You have killed at least a dozen of my patients. And you have reduced me to dementia. And how? That's the thing I can't quite pin down.

ELENA You don't sound too demented to me.

ASTROV On the verge — on the very verge, as you well know. And had you stayed you mightn't have emerged intact either. So. Who would believe it? Kharkov Of All Places saved us both! Off you go. Finita la commedia!

She takes a pencil from his table.

ELENA May I have this? A memento.

ASTROV And since we won't meet again, may I kiss you — chastely — before Vanya stumbles in with another bunch of roses? May I? (*Kisses her cheek*) You smell of lilac.

ELENA I wish you great, great happiness, Mikhail. You know that. And when I remember this summer —

She tails off. They look at each other for a few seconds.

Then quickly, passionately they kiss and embrace.

ASTROV   Stay, Elena.
ELENA   Oh, God, Mikhail —
ASTROV   Don't go.
ELENA   I must — for God's sake —

She breaks away. He tries to hold her again.

  Someone's coming. I'm off.
ASTROV   Ah! La farsa!

His exclamation and his outstretched arms include
SEREBRYAKOV, VANYA, MARIA, SONYA *and* TELEGIN
— all of whom now enter.

SEREBRYAKOV   (*To* VANYA) It's over and done with and forgotten
already. We're both sorry and that's as it should
be. And I'll tell you something, Vanya: I've
learned a lot from the experiences of the past few
hours. Might even be a paper in it.
VANYA   I'll send you the same amount as before; every
month.
SEREBRYAKOV   Splendid. 'Art and the Art of Living.'
VANYA   Everything will be the same.
SEREBRYAKOV   Something here, maybe. 'Living as an Art Form'
— what about that?

MARIA *thrusts her new pamphlet into* ASTROV'S
face.

MARIA   Brilliant! Altogether brilliant! Rosimov, the anarchist. No prisoners taken. Everybody is —

*She draws an imaginary knife across her throat and
plunges into the pamphlet again.*

ASTROV   Good. I'm all for that.

ELENA *embraces* SONYA.

SONYA Thank you for everything.

ELENA Thank *you* for everything.

SONYA Only for you I'd still be wandering around in a daze. Stupid Sonya.

ELENA Take care of yourself.

SEREBRYAKOV *kisses* MARIA's *hand.*

SEREBRYAKOV You are a truly wonderful woman. (*Shouts and points at her*) Wonderful!

MARIA Just a deaf, old gladiator. Have another formal photograph taken and send it to me, will you?

SEREBRYAKOV (*Nodding 'yes'*) 'Bye, Maman.

MARIA In your full academic regalia. God bless you. You are a good man.

SEREBRYAKOV *holds out his hand to* TELEGIN.

SEREBRYAKOV Friend. Farewell.

TELEGIN Looked Kharkov up in the encyclopaedia.

ASTROV Of all places.

TELEGIN (*To* ASTROV) Where should I have looked?

SEREBRYAKOV And — ?

TELEGIN Population of two hundred thousand. Your climate is temperate — no sweating, no freezing. Ideal.

SEREBRYAKOV Splendid.

TELEGIN And a very large colony of Germans.

SEREBRYAKOV Why would that be?

TELEGIN Your German wouldn't settle there if it wasn't a great place.

SEREBRYAKOV Would he not?

TELEGIN Your German? Professor!

SEREBRYAKOV I'm sure you're right.

TELEGIN So — a dip up, Professor!

SEREBRYAKOV (*Totally puzzled*) Indeed — Would you see that our trunks are all loaded?

TELEGIN Pleasure. Kharkov? — If you ask me, top dip!

As TELEGIN *exits* ASTROV *calls after him:*

ASTROV Ask them to bring my carriage round too, Waffles — will you?
TELEGIN (*Salutes*) Jawöhl, mein Herr — as we say.

SEREBRYAKOV *embraces and kisses* SONYA.

SEREBRYAKOV And Sonya!
SONYA Father.
SEREBRYAKOV Thank you for a thousand kindnesses.
SONYA You're looking stronger.
SEREBRYAKOV (*Whispers*) Facade. The pain is hell — (*Now aloud to* ASTROV) despite the best attentions of our friend here. Goodbye, Doctor. I've enjoyed your company enormously.
ASTROV Very kind of you.
SEREBRYAKOV Your enthusiasms, your social awareness, your passion for reform — inspiring and instructive.
ASTROV Boring at times. I know.

SEREBRYAKOV *now includes everybody.*

SEREBRYAKOV But you'll pardon an old man if he offers you all a final piece of advice. Theory is necessary. Talking has its place. But — with deference — the time for talking is over. Now you have all got to get down to real work. Roll up your sleeves. Action! The blessing of the Almighty on you all.
MARIA Hear – hear!

And the PROFESSOR *exits with a flourish, followed by* MARIA *and* SONYA.

ASTROV So there!

VANYA *takes* ELENA's *hand and kisses it.*

VANYA I'm sorry. Forgive me.

ELENA Vanya —

VANYA I'll never see you again — I know that — I do know that — but how can I —

He cannot go on. ELENA *takes his face in both her hands and kisses the top of his head.*

ELENA Lovely man. Goodbye.

She exits. Only ASTROV *and* VANYA *are left.* ASTROV *takes his paints and pencils off his desk and puts them in his bag.*

ASTROV Aren't you going to see them off?

VANYA Not feeling very well. (*He shuffles the pile of papers on his desk*) And work has to be done. He's an oaf but he's right about that — real work — action —

The sound of harness bells off.

ASTROV There they go. I'll tell you something: the oaf is one happy man. You won't find him back here in a hurry.

MARINA *enters with her knitting.*

MARINA They're gone.

ASTROV Yes. Time I moved, too.

SONYA *enters. She has been crying.*

SONYA They're gone.

ASTROV Yes.

SONYA Please God they'll be all right. Now, Uncle Vanya —

VANYA Sorry? — What's that? — Sorry? —

She lights the lamp.

SONYA   What about us getting down to some work?

VANYA   Indeed — work — indeed —

SONYA   We haven't sat together at this table for God knows how long. Even the ink-well has dried up! — that shows you. (*She fills the ink-well from a bottle in the cupboard*) Sad to see them go, isn't it?

MARIA *enters with her pamphlet.*

MARIA   They're gone.

ASTROV   Yes.

She thrusts the pamphlet into his face.

MARIA   The anarchist, Rosimov.

ASTROV   Ah.

MARIA   (*With delight*) Merciless.

ASTROV   You've told me.

MARIA   What's that?

ASTROV   (*Shouts*) Merciless? Absolutely!

MARIA   Absolutely!

MARIA *sits down and begins to read her pamphlet. Soon she falls asleep and the pamphlet drops to the ground.* SONYA *sits beside* VANYA *at the table.*

SONYA   We'll tackle the bills from the suppliers first. Some of them are final demands. Let's start with this bundle. Here — you take that half.

VANYA   (*Reads*) 'Lipski and Sons. Six coils of barbed wire delivered on — '

SONYA   The name on the left-hand column — goods next — cost on the right.

VANYA   I know.

SONYA   As we've always done it.

VANYA   I know, Sonya, I know.

MARINA *stretches and yawns.*

MARINA Well — I'm for bed.

ASTROV The excitement too much for you, Nanny?

MARINA And you should stay the night.

ASTROV Crickets chirping — pens scratching — warmth and contentment — I should, shouldn't I?

MARINA Your bed's still made up.

Harness bells off.

ASTROV Destiny (*bells*). Nothing for it but to take my belongings and my leave.

ASTROV *puts his maps into a portfolio. Neither* SONYA *nor* VANYA *appears to be aware that he is about to leave.*

ASTROV At least you'll miss me, table, won't you?

VANYA (*To* SONYA) What's that word?

SONYA Stirrup.

VANYA Looks like 'Strumpet'.

SONYA It's from Brookman, the saddler.

VANYA Ah.

They continue working. The LABOURER *enters.*

LABOURER The horses are here, Doctor.

ASTROV Take these out (*medical bag, suitcase, portfolio*). And watch you don't squash that (*portfolio*).

LABOURER I'll be careful.

ASTROV I'll be out in a minute.

ASTROV *goes to the table where* SONYA *and* VANYA *are working.*

So —

SONYA *gets to her feet.* VANYA *rises, too. Pause.*

SONYA So —

ASTROV Time to go home — or whatever that destination is called.

SONYA When will we see you again?

ASTROV Probably not before next summer. You know these roads in winter.

SONYA Yes.

ASTROV But if you need me for anything — anything at all — I'm only a four-hour drive away.

SONYA Thank you.

He takes her hand and shakes it briskly.

ASTROV Thank you for all the hospitality and the hundred-and-one kindnesses. Greatly appreciated. I'm off, Vanya.

VANYA Yes?

ASTROV You'll have your room to yourself again.

VANYA I suppose so —

ASTROV (*Shakes his hand*) Thank you for having me.

VANYA Welcome.

ASTROV You could do with a sleep too. 'Come let's to bed / says Sleepy-head.' I enjoyed that night.

VANYA What night was that?

MARINA Before you go you'll have a cup of tea.

ASTROV No, thanks, Nanny.

MARINA Vodka, maybe?

ASTROV Good God, no!

MARINA Little small one?

ASTROV What do you think?

MARINA Just a drop. It's a long journey.

ASTROV A large drop then. (*To* SONYA) Resolute to the end — that's Mikhail.

While MARINA *gets a drink from the shelf,* ASTROV, SONYA *and* VANYA *stand around in uneasy silence.* MARIA *is snoring.*

Great winter room this. The walls must be two feet thick. (*He stands in front of the map of Africa*)

That's where we should all go for the winter —
Africa.

SONYA Don't know how that map ever got there. (*To*
VANYA) Do you?

VANYA No.

ASTROV Telegin, if you ask me. Coded messages about
temperatures and climates and wonderful
German settlements over here in the East.
(*Accepting drink from* MARINA) You are an angel.

*He swallows the drink quickly and kisses the top of
her head.*

You have kept me alive all summer. (*To* ALL) I
know the way. No escort, please. And again —
thank you all — for everything. Say goodbye
to the gladiator (*Maria*) for me, will you? 'Bye.
Absolutely.

SONYA I'll see you out.

She picks up a candle and goes off behind him.
VANYA *goes back to his desk.*

VANYA What date is this, Nanny?

MARINA Is it the seventeenth or the eighteenth?

VANYA It must be.

MARINA I don't know which, though.

VANYA I'm sure you're right. Thank you.

Harness bells off.

MARINA He's gone.

VANYA Yes.

MARINA Should have stayed the night.

SONYA *enters. She joins* VANYA *at the table.*

SONYA He's gone.

VANYA Yes.

SONYA Would you like a cushion at your back?

VANYA I'm fine thanks. (*Reads*) February second — three hundred fencing-posts. February sixteenth — four hundred fencing-posts. February twenty-fourth — three hundred fencing-posts. What could we have done with a thousand fencing-posts all in the one month? Something wrong with that.

SONYA Show me.

TELEGIN *enters and sits at the door. He tunes his guitar.*

MARINA (*To* TELEGIN) What am I sitting here for? — I want to go to bed. 'Now I lay me down to sleep / I pray the Lord my soul to keep.'

TELEGIN He's gone — the Doctor?

MARINA Just missed him.

TELEGIN Do you think I'm bitter, Marina?

MARINA You? What have you to be bitter about?

TELEGIN You're right. Nothing at all. Not a thing.

SONYA (*Hands paper back*) They are Februaries in three different years, Vanya.

VANYA Ah.

They begin writing again.

MARINA 'And if I die before I wake / I pray the Lord my soul to take.' Amen.

VANYA *puts his pen down and strokes the back of* SONYA's *head.*

VANYA I am so unhappy, Sonya. If only you knew how unhappy I am.

SONYA I do know. But we must endure, Vanya. We have got to go on living and working through long, long days and long, long nights until the very end; and when our time comes we will submit to that, too, without complaining. And we will tell God that we worked as hard as we could and that we suffered and we cried and that there were times when we could hardly hold on; and He will understand and have pity on us. And then, sweet Uncle Vanya, then we will be offered a new life that will be beautiful and full of peace and full of wonder. We will be so happy, Uncle Vanya, so happy that we will look back on this life and we will smile at all the unhappiness we endured here; because we will be peaceful then, Uncle Vanya, fully peaceful, finally peaceful. I know we will. I believe that with all my heart and with all my soul.

She takes him in her arms as if he were a child. YEFIM, *off, sings a haunting folk-song.*

And I believe, too, that the angels will sing for us and the sky will be festooned with stars as bright as diamonds and all the misery of this life, all the terrible things we've had to endure, they will be swept away in a great wave of mercy and understanding. And for the first time ever we will know what it is to be peaceful and at rest.

She wipes away his tears. She is on the verge of tears herself.

Poor Uncle Vanya; God help you; you're crying. You've had a very unhappy life — I do know that. But be patient. Endure. And peace will come to us. Listen to me, Uncle Vanya. Believe me. Peace will come to us.

She kisses the top of his head. Then they pick up their pens and begin writing. Silence — except for the scraping pens, the crickets, YEFIM, *off.*